HARNESSING YOUR EMOTIONS

Andrew Wommack

Harnessing Your Emotions
ISBN 978-1-60683-526-5
Copyright © 2009 by Andrew Wommack

Published in Partnership

Andrew Wommack Ministries
P.O. Box 3333
Colorado Springs, CO 80934-3333

Harrison House Publishing

Contents

Introduction

When I was growing up, I was painfully shy, fearful, and timid, which are all negative emotions. They were things I needed to be delivered from. But even though I had emotional problems, I never went through severe depression. I never experienced the extremes that some people talk about.

On March 23, 1968 I had a personal encounter with the Lord. I was born again at the age of eight, but at the age of eighteen I had an encounter with God in which He poured out His love upon me in such a tangible way that it radically changed my life. For four and a half months, I was so caught up in the awareness of God's presence, His love for me, and His acceptance of me that it overwhelmed me. It was a radical, awesome, life-changing experience. Most people would think, *Well, then, after that you must have lived happily ever after.*

Yes, it was a wonderful experience, but it wore off. After four and a half months, I lost that feeling—that emotion of God's love for me and His presence with me. When it left, I went through a time of discouragement that was worse than anything I had ever known in my life. My dad died when I was a young child, and all kinds of negative things happened to me in my early life. But those things were nothing compared to what I felt when the knowledge of God's love and presence left me.

I was in Vietnam at the time, in a very negative situation. I was so hungry to regain the presence of the Lord, I spent months asking God to kill me—not because I was in sin and not because of my physical circumstances. It was because I had tasted of a love and a relationship with God that I just felt I could not live without. It was like being on a high, and when I came down I asked myself how I could ever again live at a level below that.

Now, the point that I am making is that the severest depression I have ever experienced came not because of sin or of problems in the physical, natural realm, but because I had a longing for God that I was no longer able to fulfill.

Some people get depressed and discouraged, because they are caught up in the world. They dwell on things they should not be thinking about, or they do not recognize the priority that God should have in their lives. But that is not the only reason people have emotional problems. Even those who are born again, filled with the Spirit of God, and trying to live a Christian life can experience emotional problems.

We will be taking a look at why we have emotional problems, what solutions the world offers versus those the Word of God offers, and why God's answers bring lasting results. God has equipped us through His Word to control our emotions—good and bad. We can walk in true emotional stability each and every day of our lives if our faith and trust is in Him.

Chapter 1

God's Attitude
toward Emotions

According to the *American Heritage Dictionary*, the word *harness* means "to bring under control and direct the force of." I believe that is really descriptive of the way the Lord would have us deal with our emotions. He wants us to harness, to control, and to direct the force of our emotions.

We cannot deny that emotions exist, and yet some people, because of the negative experiences they've had with their emotions, go to the extreme and try to become emotionless. They try to just quit feeling anything. I see this happen many times with pastors who have gotten close to someone in their church and been hurt because that person left them or turned on them, which is very common. I would say that a large percentage of ministers, because of such negative emotional experiences, simply withdraw and never get close to anyone again. They don't develop close friendships, because of a fear of being hurt. They may avoid some hurts, but they also miss out on one of God's greatest blessings.

God created us with emotions, and it's wrong to try to become emotionless, to withdraw to a state in which nothing ever bothers us—a state in which we are just numb. That is certainly not what God wants. We were created with emotions, and we are to enjoy those emotions.

God Himself is a God of emotion. First John 4:8 tells us that God is love, which is an emotion. It's not only an emotion, but it involves emotion. The Bible also says in many different places that the Lord is a jealous God, and that He can be angry. In Ephesians 4:30, it says we can grieve the Holy Spirit. All of these are emotions.

Emotions Are Meant for Enjoyment

I believe it is a wrong reaction when we try not to have any kind of emotional relationship with anyone because of the potential damage. That is an attempt to deny emotions, to deny that they exist, and I believe that is working against the framework, the very makeup we were created with.

We were created in God's image, and part of that likeness of God is emotions. God gave them to us to be enjoyed. When God created the world, He looked at everything He made and said, **"Behold, it was good"** (Gen. 1:31). So emotions were created to be good. I believe that emotions are one of the spices of life that really make it worth living. If there was no love in our lives, if there was no joy, what would be the point of being alive? Just think what life would be like if we were to erase every memory of positive emotions, such as the memories of great times we have had. It would radically alter our existence.

At the same time, even though emotions are intended to be good and God gave them to us to be enjoyed, many people find that their emotions are out of control. Instead of controlling their emotions, their emotions are controlling them. Even though emotions were intended to be a positive thing, they can also be the very thing that drives people to depression, which causes all kinds of problems: divorce, anger, bitterness, hurt feelings, and even suicide.

Finding Hope for Emotional Stability

I feel that the world is basically hopeless in the area of emotions. Because they have no real hope, many secular psychologists just try to make people feel better by telling them they shouldn't worry about their lack of emotional stability. They say they shouldn't look at themselves as being abnormal, because everyone else is as bad off as they are. That's a feeble answer.

It is surprising that the church, the Christian community, has really not taught very much in the area of emotional stability. I feel that most of the teaching that comes forth from the church deals with *coping* rather than *controlling*. Instead of teaching people how to have victory in this area, the church teaches them to "roll with the punches" and tells them to "learn something" from their emotions. There may be some benefit in that, but nothing lasting. With God's help, people cannot only learn to cope and survive; they can learn to hope and thrive in this area of emotions.

I travel around the country teaching a lot on emotions. In my meetings, I often give an invitation asking people to stand up for prayer who have been fighting depression and losing the battle. It's not unusual to see close to 80 percent of the Christians in those meetings standing for prayer. Many times the number goes up to 90 percent. Sometimes it looks like the entire congregation is standing!

Please do not misunderstand me. I am not condemning those people. I understand their struggle, and I have compassion for them. I pray for them, but I know that is *not* the way Jesus intended for them to live. The Lord came to deliver not only our eternal spiritual man but also our soulish, emotional personality. Jesus paid for that at the cross.

Mental and emotional health is a part of what Jesus came to bring. There are truths and instruction in God's Word that if followed and applied, I unconditionally guarantee will cause you to live an emotionally stable life.

You don't have to have extreme highs and extreme lows. You can live on an even plane of continual joy and peace. Isaiah 26:3 says that the Lord will keep him in perfect peace whose mind is stayed upon Him because he trusts in Him. Well, peace is an emotion, and you can live in a state of perfect emotional peace.

Responsibility for Emotions

> **Moreover all these curses shall come upon thee, and shall pursue thee, and overtake thee, till thou be destroyed; because thou hearkenedst not unto the voice of the LORD thy God, to keep his commandments and his statutes which he commanded thee:**
> **And they shall be upon thee for a sign and for a wonder, and upon thy seed for ever.**
> **Because thou servedst not the LORD thy God with joyfulness, and with gladness of heart, for the abundance of all things;**
> **Therefore shalt thou serve thine enemies which the LORD shall send against thee, in hunger, and in thirst, and in nakedness, and in want of all things: and he shall put a yoke of iron upon thy neck, until he have destroyed thee.**
> *Deuteronomy 28:45-48*

Here is a passage of Scripture most people have either never seen or never applied to the area of emotions. In this passage, the Lord was talking to the nation of Israel, telling them that because they had not done certain things, He was going to bring judgment upon them. This judgment was the result of their acts of sin.

In the Old Testament, God judged sin harshly. In the New Testament, our judgment has been placed upon Jesus, so even though we don't always do what we should, God does not judge us. But we can still benefit from seeing what the Lord judged as wrong conduct.

In this passage, God made an awesome statement. He said that He was bringing judgment upon His people because they did not serve Him with joyfulness and gladness of heart for the abundance of all of the things He had given them. Most people read it and say, "Yes, God hated sin and judged it." But this passage shows that God not only hated sin; He hated negative emotions. It was because His people had not served Him with their *emotions* that He was bringing judgment upon them.

Very few people see emotions in that light. Most people look at emotions as being optional. They would like to have positive emotions, but they don't feel responsible for producing them. I don't know anyone who gets up in the morning and prays, "O God, help me to have a bad day. I want to be bummed out and depressed to the max." No one desires that. Yet when certain things happen and they begin to *feel* that way, they don't feel guilty. They don't feel they have done anything wrong. Instead, they feel justified.

When people come to me for counseling and I begin telling them what God desires for them, they immediately respond, "But look at what has happened to me." They start telling me about all their negative experiences. Their thinking seems to be, *I'm justified in feeling this way because of my circumstances. How else can I feel?*

Most people believe that if something negative happens, there must be a negative emotion to correspond with it. They see emotions as simply a response, not a choice. To them, emotions are not something they have any authority or control over; therefore, they have no responsibility for them.

Emotions are just something that happen. That's the current thinking of our day. Yet that cannot be true, or God would have been unjust to bring judgment upon the nation of Israel because they did not serve Him with their emotions. It would be unjust for God to hold us accountable for something we had no control over.

Let Not Your Heart Be Troubled

Let not your heart be troubled.

John 14:1

On the very night before His crucifixion, Jesus spoke to His disciples and told them not to let their hearts be troubled. That wasn't a suggestion; it was a command. Jesus wasn't speaking to those men in a time of prosperity and peace when everything was going great. Most people feel that when everything is going fine, they should be praising God and operating in joy and peace. When negative things come, they act as though they have some responsibility for their emotions. But when *big* problems come, they think that relieves them of *all* responsibility for their emotions: *No one can be expected to overcome in this situation!*

The Lord was talking to His disciples just before they would face a tremendous trial. He knew that what they were going to experience was greater than anything they had ever known. He knew they were going to see what they considered their whole lives—their whole calling and everything they had sacrificed for— crucified, destroyed, and defeated. He knew they weren't going to understand what was happening to them in that terribly trying time. Yet He told them, "Don't let your hearts be troubled."

Jesus would be unjust to give someone a command like that if that individual did not have the power to do what He said. Those disciples did have the power to keep their hearts from being troubled. They didn't exercise it, and the Lord wound up forgiving them, ministering to them, and comforting them. But His best was for them to put their trust in Him and not let their hearts be troubled.

I am not trying to put condemnation on anyone, but I am saying that before we can really start experiencing victory in this area of harnessing our emotions, we are going to have to get rid of the lie that we have no authority over our emotions. Emotions are not just something that happen to us like a chemical reaction we have no ability to control. We are not like animals that just respond to their environments. We are people created in the image of God who have the power of choice (Deut. 30:19). We do have authority over our emotions through Jesus Christ, and it is time to walk in that authority and take control of our feelings.

Natural versus Supernatural

Now, if someone is hateful toward us or comes against us, it's normal to feel hurt and rejected. That is a natural human response. But we don't have to live under the control of the natural; we can live supernaturally.

If you are born again and Jesus Christ has changed you on the inside, then you have the ability to supersede natural law. You can bring your emotions under the spiritual dominion of Christ rather than under the physical dominion of the world.

I don't believe that God intends for us to live by what the natural realm dictates. This is one of the fundamental, foundational differences between biblical emotional stability and secular psychological stability. Psychology does not factor God into the equation. The word "psychology" comes from a root word *psyche*, which was the name of a Greek deity—the god of the soul. Psychology deals with the emotional and mental realm. It doesn't take into account the spiritual man. It tries to solve problems from a purely natural, physical standpoint, not from the standpoint of the supernatural ability of God.

Another word for this approach is *humanism*. In other words, we have all the answers within ourselves; we don't need God.

According to humanistic philosophy, the answer to our problems is not found in the spiritual part of us, but in the mental and emotional part. That is totally wrong. God created mankind in His likeness and in His image, which is spiritual (Gen. 1:26-27). God created us to be dependent upon Him. He did not create us to be stand-alone people. We must be in relationship and in communion with Him to be spiritually healthy.

All of our problems began when we separated ourselves from God and began to do our own thing and make our own decisions. That's when all the corruption came into the world. Psychology does not recognize that truth. Based purely on secular principles, psychology does not see God as the force of life with the power to overcome and change emotions. Instead, psychology tries to bring about solutions through manipulation in the physical, emotional realm of the mind. That is different from the way Christians are to operate. We should not accept natural things as being normal.

Yes, it is natural for me to be hurt when someone treats me unfairly. But as a Christian, I am not just natural anymore; I have been born again. One-third of me is wall-to-wall Holy Ghost. I now have God Himself living on the inside of me, and I am not limited to natural resources. I have the divine, supernatural ability of God on the inside of me. It would be just plain stupid of me not to draw on God's power and to only look at things as they are and try to learn to cope with them.

As Christians, we are not to look at the unbelievers around us to see how they are living and expect the same thing for ourselves. I expect more because I have more. God has done a miraculous thing in my life, and if you're born again, God has done the same thing for you.

Accountability for Emotions

> **Be careful for nothing; but in every thing by prayer and supplication with thanksgiving let your requests be made known unto God.**
>
> **And the peace of God, which passeth all understanding, shall keep your hearts and minds through Christ Jesus.**
>
> *Philippians 4:6-7*

We are accountable for our emotions. God has given us the ability to control this area of our lives. If He hadn't, He would be unjust to bring judgment on us for having negative emotions. He would be unjust to command us to do something we cannot do—to react positively to the negative experiences of this life.

As we saw in John 14:1, the Lord doesn't expect us to have positive emotions only when everything is going our way. In John 16:33, Jesus said to His disciples, **"In the world ye shall have tribulation: but be of good cheer; I have overcome the world."** When we are facing trials and tribulation, we are commanded to be of good cheer because Jesus has overcome the world.

The Lord has given us the power to control our emotional reactions to whatever comes against us. Our emotional stability should not depend upon our circumstances or on how things are going. God's kind of peace is based totally upon Him. It's just a matter of keeping our eyes stayed on Him and walking in faith. If we can access the supernatural power and ability of God, it doesn't matter what's going on in the physical realm.

Many people think, *If I could just change my mate; if my kids weren't rebellious; if I had a different job; if I had more money; if this or that or the other, then I would have emotional happiness.* That is a lie that Satan uses to keep people in the mess they're in instead of just totally surrendering and saying, "God, help me." The devil keeps people thinking, *Man, if this situation will just change, everything will be all right.* But that's not true. It's not our circumstances that are the problem; it's how we are reacting to them that causes us grief. Now, I am not saying that circumstances aren't a factor. Satan uses them against us, but we can overcome all those things.

> **If I ascend up into heaven, thou art there: if I make my bed in hell, behold, thou art there.**
>
> ***Psalm 139:8***

Wherever you are and whatever you are going through, God is there. It doesn't matter what your situation is. You may be in a living hell, but if your mind is focused on God and the great things He has done for you, you can have joy and peace in the midst of that situation. There are literally thousands of examples in God's Word of that very thing. I know from my own experiences that joy and peace can reign in the midst of terrible circumstances. If you are honest, you can look back over your life and remember times that in the natural realm, things seemed to be falling apart. Yet when you turned to God and called out to Him, the Lord gave you the peace that passes all understanding—a supernatural peace (Phil. 4:6-7).

Such a peace is beyond physical explanation. There may not have been anything in the natural to make you feel good, but because you cried out to God, you experienced His supernatural peace. You can do that at any time and in any situation. Your circumstances are not an excuse for being defeated, depressed, helpless, or hopeless.

There is no natural thing and no physical thing that can stop you from experiencing the joy and the peace God intended for you to have. It is yours. It already belongs to you. It has your name on it. If you will get your thinking straightened out, you can begin to access that joy and peace regardless of your problems.

Don't wait until something in the natural changes. It is when you begin to change your heart attitude that you will begin to bring your emotions under control. When you change your heart attitude, you will have emotional stability, no matter what your circumstances may be.

The Source of Temptation

Let no man say when he is tempted, I am tempted of God: for God cannot be tempted with evil, neither tempteth he any man.

James 1:13

One of the first steps to overcome negative emotions is to say, "Father, it is not Your will that I be this way." God is not the one who makes people depressed, discouraged, angry, or bitter.

Often people blame God, thinking He has allowed some negative thing to happen to them for some mysterious, unknown reason. They say, "God must be punishing me for something I did wrong in my life, so I guess I'll just have to bear my cross and suffer for Him even though it is destroying me emotionally." God is not the one who makes people emotional wrecks. That is not the way God operates; that's the way Satan operates.

The Cause of Temptation

But every man is tempted, when he is drawn away of his own lust, and enticed.

James 1:14

Lust

When this verse says "every man," it means there is no exception. This is a universal truth that applies in every situation to all mankind, men and women alike.

As I deal with people along these lines, they constantly tell me, "Well, I'm an exception. My situation's unique. You just don't understand." That's one of the deceptions Satan uses against us. This verse says that every person is drawn away by their own lust, which eventually results in sin and death.

We usually use the word *lust* to describe sexual desire or perversion. Even though it applies in that situation, the word literally refers to any type of strong emotion. In James 4:5, it is even used in a positive sense, where it says, **"The spirit that dwelleth in us lusteth to envy."** This is not talking about some kind of perversion of our old nature; it is talking about the Holy Spirit within us that longs for us jealously. The Amplified Bible translates this sentence: **"The Spirit Whom He has caused to dwell in us yearns over us and He yearns for the Spirit [to be welcome] with a jealous love."** Exodus 20:5 tells us our God is a jealous God. In Galatians 5:17, we are told that the flesh lusts against the Spirit, and the Spirit lusts against the flesh. All of these verses are talking about the Holy Spirit. So lust doesn't have to refer to some type of sexual desire. It can refer to any strong, overwhelming emotion—positive or negative.

The Results of Temptation

Then when lust hath conceived, it bringeth forth sin: and sin, when it is finished, bringeth forth death.

James 1:15

It is through lust or strong emotion that a person is tempted and drawn away into sin. Once that individual has sinned, they are subject to the wages of sin, which is death (Rom. 6:23).

Sin is *conceived* in the emotions. This verse compares sin, or the process of the development of sin, to the process of childbirth.

If a woman does not want to have a child, the time to exercise her choice is not after she has conceived so that she has to abort and take the life of an unborn infant. The time to exercise her choice is before she has the physical relationship that results in conception. It is wrong to use abortion as a form of birth control. If a woman doesn't want children, she shouldn't have the sexual relationship that produces them.

In the natural, most Christians understand that truth and see the wisdom in it. But when it comes to spiritual things, they don't understand that negative emotions are where sin is conceived. No one would ever commit the physical act of sin if they did not begin to entertain the emotions that conceive that sin on the inside of them.

Let's take the example of suicide. A person would never commit suicide if they would reject the depression that leads to it. If they would consider thoughts of depression as sin and resist those thoughts the same way they would resist the act of suicide, they would never give birth to suicide, because it would never be conceived in the womb of their emotions.

That is an awesome truth because it applies to all sin, not just abortion and suicide. Most of us look at emotions as being optional. It's nice to have good ones, but if bad ones come along, that's just the way it is. But we don't look at sin that way.

If we are tempted with thoughts about adultery, we cast down those thoughts and bring them into captivity to the obedience of

Jesus Christ (2 Cor. 10:5). We resist those thoughts because we know the physical action they lead to is wrong. We haven't put negative emotions into that same category, yet that is exactly what James 1:15 does. When we lust or when we experience negative emotions, sin is conceived right then. Unless we get a spiritual abortion along the way, we will end up acting out what we feel. Anger, bitterness, divorce, and all kinds of sins come from acting on thoughts and emotions that should never have been entertained in the first place.

<u>Importance of Emotional Control</u>

Emotions are critical because of what they produce. If we want to control sin in our lives we must control our emotions, because that is where sin is conceived. It is impossible to live a holy life and be dedicated wholly to God if our emotions are not under control.

Suppose a woman wants to remain single all her life and never have any children, yet she has no restraint on her sexual behavior and sleeps with a different man every night. Unless something is wrong with her biologically, sooner or later she is going to get pregnant and conceive a child.

We would say it's stupid to act that way, yet spiritually that's what many Christians are doing. They are allowing negative emotions to bombard them and affect their lives. Yet they think, *Well, that's normal. It's natural. That's the way everyone is.* They are, in effect, opening themselves up to problems. Those who have unrestrained relationships with negative emotions often wonder why they keep constantly conceiving sin. It's because of the thoughts and feelings they are allowing to run rampant through their minds and hearts.

Faith Produces Positive Emotions

Wherein ye greatly rejoice, though now for a season, if need be, ye are in heaviness through manifold temptations:

That the trial of your faith, being much more precious than of gold that perisheth, though it be tried with fire, might be found unto praise and honour and glory at the appearing of Jesus Christ:

Whom having not seen, ye love; in whom, though now ye see him not, yet believing, ye rejoice with joy unspeakable and full of glory.

1 Peter 1:6-8

It is not acceptable for us to have negative emotions—to be anxious, angry, bitter, or depressed—when the Lord has told us not to have them. We may be going through trials and we may not see the Lord at work in our situations, but we can rejoice with joy unspeakable and can constantly be full of glory. That's the way Christians ought to be.

Peter does not say that operating in faith is automatic. Just because we are born again does not mean we are automatically joyous and full of glory. He says that it is only when we *believe* that we can rejoice and be full of glory.

We have been given the power to operate in joy and glory, but that power has to be released through faith. One of the first steps in releasing our faith is changing our expectations. We need to quit looking at the world and saying, "Well, this is the way it is." We need to look at God's Word and say, "Hey, this is not the way God intended it to be. God intended for me to have positive emotions." We must believe that God gave us the power to change—our thoughts, our emotions, ourselves, and our circumstances—by exercising faith.

Life or Death, Blessing or Cursing

I call heaven and earth to record this day against you, that I have set before you life and death, blessing and cursing: therefore choose life, that both thou and thy seed may live.

Deuteronomy 30:19

The Lord was telling the Israelites, "I am calling heaven and earth to record against you today." That means God was saying, "Everyone listen." This was something He wanted the whole universe to know. Then He said, "I am setting before you life and death, blessing and cursing, so choose life so both you, your children, and your children's children can live and prosper."

When the Lord talked about choosing life, He was including more than just our emotions. He was talking about choosing physical life over death. God was promising the children of Israel that if they would serve Him, He would prosper them financially and bless them physically. But He also made it clear that they would suffer captivity and the ruin of their nation if they forsook Him.

Although the Lord was referring to physical life and death in this verse, He was also talking about spiritual life versus spiritual death. I really believe that an important part of the life that God desires for His children to have is emotional stability.

The thief cometh not, but for to steal, and to kill, and to destroy: I am come that they might have life, and that they might have it more abundantly.

John 10:10

Peace I leave with you, my peace I give unto you: not as the world giveth, give I unto you.

16

Let not your heart be troubled, neither let it be afraid.

John 14:27

All of this and more is part of what Jesus produced for us in His life, death, and resurrection.

When God says "Choose life," I believe that choice includes emotional stability. God gave us the choice of life or death, of peace or turmoil, of joy or fear. God will not make that choice for us. God is not the one who controls our lives and makes us miserable. No, as James tells us, each of us is tempted through our own lust. It is our own desires that bring about these negative things in our lives. (See James 1:14.) We can't even blame the devil. Satan cannot make the choice, because God said He gave it to us.

God has given us this ability to choose. We may think, *But wait a minute. I'm depressed and discouraged, and I certainly didn't choose to be this way.*

No, we didn't choose it in the sense that we said, "God, make me miserable." But we chose to think in ways and do certain things that produce negative emotions. So, yes, we did choose. It may not have been a very overt choice. It may have been subtle, but nonetheless it is because of our wrong choices that we have problems and become emotionally upset.

Don't Be Angry

Get rid of all bitterness, rage and anger.
Ephesians 4:31, NIV

Sometimes our situations or circumstances are simply the result of choosing to believe the wrong thing. Many of us believe that if a person is angry at us, we can't help but be angry back at them. If we believe that, we are going to have anger, and that anger is going to have a negative effect on our lives.

The Bible teaches that we have a choice about whether or not we will be angry at those who are angry at us. In fact, it teaches that we are to choose to control our bitterness, rage, and anger. Jesus Himself forgave the very people who were crucifying Him and mocking Him. He was able to look down upon them from the cross with love in His heart and pray, **"Father, forgive them; for they know not what they do"** (Luke 23:34). We have the ability to make that same choice every day.

<u>Choose Life</u>

One of the most distinguishing characteristics of human beings is the fact that God gave us a choice that even He Himself will not override. God says to us, "You choose." He won't make the choice for us, but He will tell us which choice to make. He says, "Choose (A) life or (B) death." (See Deuteronomy 30:19.) And then He says, "(A) is the correct answer; choose life." God is a loving Father who helps us in every way, but ultimately we are the ones who choose how we want to be.

It is not what other people do to us that causes us problems with our emotions, but what is inside of us. It's the way we choose to react to what happens to us that causes our problems. I know that may sound really far fetched, but I promise you it is true.

God gave us the choice of controlling or not controlling our emotions. We must accept that responsibility even before we learn the steps toward releasing our emotions properly. In order to use the power and ability we have been given, we have to first accept the fact that we can change. We are not just a hunk of chemicals. We are not like an animal that has no choice in the matter.

Being Spiritually Minded

For to be carnally minded is death; but to be spiritually minded is life and peace.

Romans 8:6

This verse doesn't say that being spiritually minded *tends* toward life and peace. It says to be spiritually minded *is* life and peace. There is no exception. If a person is not experiencing life and peace, they are not spiritually minded.

Spiritual–mindedness produces peace exactly the way that planting wheat seeds produces wheat. You don't plant wheat and get corn. You reap what you plant. Anyone who claims to have planted wheat but they have corn growing in their field is wrong. They may have thought they planted wheat, but their harvest proves what they planted. Likewise, your emotional harvest reveals what you've been thinking.

Being spiritually minded doesn't necessarily mean thinking about religious things all the time. In John 6:63, Jesus said, **"The words that I speak unto you, they are spirit, and they are life."** God's Word is spiritual. Thinking in line with what God's Word says produces life and peace. There are no exceptions—that's just the way it is.

Here the word *carnal* does not necessarily mean "sinful." It means physical; oriented with the flesh and the frailties of human nature; dominated by what is seen, tasted, heard, smelled, and felt. (See James Strong's, *The Exhaustive Concordance of the Bible* [Nashville: Abingdon, 1890], "Greek Dictionary of the New Testament," #4561.) If you are carnally minded, you will die, but if you are spiritually minded, you will have life and peace. Compare this verse with Deuteronomy 30:19, where God says to **"choose life, that both thou and thy seed may live."** I believe the life we are to choose includes emotionally stability, and we get that by being spiritually minded, which leads to life and peace.

Sadly, many people will never experience God's life and peace. I think there are literally millions who are hiding behind the mentality that their problems are some kind of chemical imbalance. But that's not it at all. It's not their hormones that are affecting them, and it's not the chemistry of their bodies that is making them the way they are. Scripture teaches us that as a person thinks in their heart, so are they (Prov. 23:7). I don't doubt that some people do have a chemical imbalance. I have known people who have told me that was their problem; they took a particular drug, and it changed everything in their lives. I think having a chemical imbalance is a possibility, but even if it is, it's the exception rather than the rule.

If you think that is your problem, you need to know that the answer isn't in taking a pill for the rest of your life. You can be healed. You can overcome. You can choose life—real life. The choice is yours. Choose life!

Chapter 2

Walking by Faith, Not by Emotions

For we walk by faith [we regulate our lives and conduct ourselves by our conviction or belief respecting man's relationship to God and divine things, with trust and holy fervor] thus we walk] not by sight or appearance.

2 Corinthians 5:7, AMP

Sometimes people who are living a very moral life and loving God with all of their hearts become discouraged and depressed because they are seeking something God never intended them to have. I believe I have experienced as much of an emotional high in my relationship with God as anyone else, but I have come to realize that even though that is a blessing, and I praise God for it and rejoice in it, it is not something that can be sustained twenty-four hours a day. Some people who read that statement may choke on it, thinking, *What are you saying?* I'm saying that in our relationship with the Lord, we have to learn to walk by faith and not by sight or appearance—that is, not by emotion.

In my own life, I had to make that transition from emotion to faith. When I was in Vietnam, I literally got to a place where I knew God wasn't going to kill me, and even though I begged Him to, I had to go on living despite my feelings. So I just started saying, "God, what am I going to do?" I knew I couldn't just sit there and twiddle my thumbs. If I did, I would be pulled in the direction of the world. I had to start doing something, and out of desperation I began studying the Word for up to sixteen hours a day. I started reading it just to keep out of trouble and to keep my mind stayed on God. As I did, I started making a transition from the emotion of *feeling* God's love to the faith of *knowing* God's love. God's Word began to give me the satisfaction and the stability that in the past, I had looked to my emotions to provide.

move from feeling God's love to knowing God's love

Faith Is a Product of the Heart

God wants us to live by faith in Him, not by our emotions. Emotions tend to be dependent on our circumstances, which is the physical realm. Faith is a product of the heart, which is the spiritual realm.

Emotions can be touched by the devil. When negative things happen to us, we are going to be affected emotionally. There will be a fluctuation in our emotional state. But spiritual truths are eternal. When we start walking by faith instead of by feelings, we will be much more mature and stable.

The person who goes by the fact that they know God loves them because they have educated themselves through His Word and have based their life on it will sacrifice everything they have for the Word. That person will have a superior walk to the individual who has a great relationship with God based on emotions. As soon as something goes wrong, the emotional person will start saying, "Has God left me? Has He quit loving me? Is He displeased with me for some reason?" They will end up on an emotional roller coaster, wondering what has happened and why God has seemingly forsaken them.

Sometimes I see more stability in denominational people who have not received the baptism of the Holy Spirit than I do in some Spirit-filled people. The reason is because they are basing their lives on God's unchanging Word and not on their fluctuating emotions.

<u>Danger of Emotional Addiction</u>

I have experienced the baptism of the Holy Spirit. I am all for it. I advocate it. But I am aware of the danger of emotional attachment to any experience in life, no matter how good or godly it may be. When a person receives the baptism of the Holy Ghost, there is a tremendous emotional experience that goes along with it, and that can become a problem if it is not properly understood.

When I was born again at the age of eight, I accepted the Lord by faith. I received much of the benefit of my new relationship with Him then. But as far as having the Lord involved in every single thing in my life, that didn't come until I was eighteen, when I was baptized in the Holy Spirit. When that happened, such an emotion came over me that I suddenly knew beyond a shadow of a doubt that God was real and alive. I could close my eyes at any time and visualize Him right there in front of me. It was almost as if I could reach out and touch Him. There was a reality, an emotion, and a feeling to it.

But because of that experience, there was a temptation for me to become addicted to that emotion in a way that I had never been tempted in my life. Before I experienced the overwhelming emotion that comes with the knowledge of God's love and presence, I didn't know what I was missing. I just thought everyone went through life the way I did. But once I had that emotional experience, it was like taking dope. It gave me such a high that I felt like I would sell my own mother to have another feeling like that.

I believe there are many people who have had a miraculous encounter with the Lord and who have allowed themselves to become addicted to the emotion that often accompanies that experience. They reject the negative emotions of depression and other such feelings that arise from carnal things, but when it comes to their relationship with God, they feel that something is wrong unless they are on a continual emotional high. I meet Christians all the time who are depressed and discouraged, not because of sin in their lives, but because they're always seeking some emotional "fix."

Emotional times do come and we should praise God for them, but we can't live on that level. I don't believe God wants us to be on a constant search for emotional highs. He would much rather have us walk by faith, whether there is any emotion attached to it or not. That is what is known as emotional stability.

Emotional Maturity

When my wife and I first got married, the emotional love we had between us was just awesome. We couldn't think of anything or anyone else but each other. We would just sit and look at one another nearly twenty-four hours a day. All we wanted was to be with each other, and that's great. There's nothing wrong with that— for newlyweds.

But now that we've been married for nearly forty years, things have changed. My wife and I love each other infinitely more today than we did then. Our love is deeper, richer, and stronger, and yes, it's different. I can go to the office all day now and not fall apart emotionally, thinking, *Man, I can't stand it! I've got to get back to my wife.*

Emotions have become such a part of life today that some people think, *Well, that's the way it should be. You should be so much in love that you just can't function without thinking about your wife.* I don't believe that's the way God made us to be. I enjoy my wife and I cherish her. I love her more now than I ever have, and through the years, our emotions have matured. They are not the same.

When I first fell in love with Jamie, she could just walk into the room, and my heart would do flip-flops. I felt that if we were separated, I would die. If I were still functioning that way today, I wouldn't be worth two cents. I couldn't go anywhere to minister to others. I surely couldn't go overseas and leave her for a week or two at a time. I wouldn't be worth anything to the Lord.

I know a couple who are very happily married now, yet an overly developed emotional tie by the wife threatened their marriage in the beginning. The woman had been married before to a man who abused her both physically and emotionally. Therefore, when she married this godly man, she clung to him desperately. She became codependent on him in such a way that he couldn't function. She demanded all his attention.

Finally he sat her down and told her how much he loved her. He assured her that he would never leave her and that he desired her more than any person or thing in the world. Then he dropped the bomb. He said, "But I don't need you."

He wasn't rejecting her; he was expressing the fact that he was a complete person based on his relationship with the Lord alone. He loved his wife and was committed to her, but he didn't fall apart like a two-dollar suitcase every time she did something that displeased him. In her own words, she told me that was the beginning of a mighty healing in her that ultimately saved their marriage.

God didn't design us to be totally emotionally dependent on anyone but Him. Does that mean that we should never have feelings for our spouses or that when we fall in love, we should be totally emotionless? No, I don't believe that at all. I think emotion in romantic love is great and should be enjoyed, even after twenty years. But we should recognize the fact that as time goes on, there is going to be a maturing process. Love is not all emotions.

The Maturing Process

The same principle of the maturing process in our relationship with people applies to our relationship with God. I have had some awesome experiences with the Lord. I had one experience in

Vietnam when I was suddenly caught up in His presence. I don't know if I was in my body or out of it. All I know is that I was so overwhelmed, I forgot everything physical. When I finally came to, I found myself covered with hundreds and hundreds of cockroaches swarming me and biting me. I had welts all over me, but I didn't even feel the physical pain, because I was so caught up in that spiritual experience.

I haven't had an experience quite like that one since. Does that mean my relationship with God has gone downhill since then? No, it just means it's different now. If I ever have an experience like that again, it will be great, but I'm not seeking it. It's not even my desire. I have now come to the place where I *know* God loves me, so I don't need an experience to make me *feel* that He loves me. Those emotional times do come and I certainly enjoy them, but I don't *need* them in the sense that I doubt God's love for me if there aren't strong emotions. *I don't need the emotion to know God loves me*

If there were two doors set in front of Christians today, one marked "emotions" and the other marked "faith," I am convinced that most believers would choose the one marked "emotions." Yet the Bible teaches that *faith* is the victory that overcomes the world (1 John 5:4). Without *faith* it is impossible to please God (Heb. 11:6). What we in the church of Jesus Christ need today is not less emotions, but more faith.

I am not opposed to emotions. I have them and I enjoy them, but they do not rule over me and control my life. Even if I never feel a thing, I still know God loves me, and that knowledge gives me peace and joy. I operate from a secure knowledge, not from some vague feeling that cannot be grabbed hold of because there's no handle on it and no way to control it.

When I begin to experience negative emotions, I go back to what God has told me in His Word. I let the knowledge of God's Word change my emotions. If you will do that, I promise you it will help you gain stability in this vital area of your life.

Bridle Your Emotions

As we mature spiritually, we'll also see a maturing take place in the natural. One of the most obvious is in the area of our emotions. Controlled emotions will be the result of spiritual maturity.

I have had horses for a long time. I enjoy them and have a great time with them. I'm not a great horseman, but I have learned some things along the way about horses. There are some truths about them that apply to emotions as well.

A horse is a very strong, powerful animal—much stronger than a human being. The average horse weighs somewhere between a thousand and two thousand pounds. It's a huge animal with tremendous strength. Today horses have largely been replaced by machines and vehicles, but in recent history, a horse was not just something for fun and entertainment; it was an essential.

Horses have played a very important part in history and in the development of civilization. They have enabled armies to win battles. They have given people more power, more mobility, and more strength than they could ever have had on their own. They have enabled people to do things they could never have done in their own physical ability.

So a horse is a powerful force, but at the same time, a horse has to be managed. A horse that is out of control can cause a great deal of destruction. I know that is true from personal experience.

Emotions are the same way. Under control, they make life great. They increase effectiveness and provide a great deal of satisfaction and joy. But out of control, emotions can be devastating.

We see examples of this constantly in the news media as we hear of people who are battling depression or some other negative emotion. There we learn about the tragic effect it is having on them. Emotions breed many problems in our society and in our personal lives.

So, like a horse, emotions are powerful. They can be tremendously beneficial, or they can be extremely destructive—even deadly. That is why, like a horse, they need to be bridled.

Psychology versus Spirituality

Much of our attitudes today about emotions have been polluted by psychology. It is not my purpose to attack psychology or psychologists. My purpose is to establish the truth of what God's Word says about emotions. I know there are many Christian psychologists and Christian psychological therapy centers established throughout the United States. I believe psychology can be of great benefit in certain cases, but I also believe there are some things psychology teaches that are diametrically opposed to what God's Word teaches.

To a large degree, psychology has not really taught us how to manage, harness, or control our emotions. Instead, it has taught us to give vent to our emotions and to simply allow them to run their course in our lives. Psychology has said, in essence, "Don't feel bad for feeling this way. Don't hold anything in. Let it all out." This is like strapping a person on a horse and telling them just to hold on while the horse runs and bucks, but giving them no bridle, bit, or reins to control the horse. In my estimation, that is completely irresponsible.

If you don't know how to control a horse, you don't have any business being on one. If you don't know how to control your emotions, you are in just as much danger as an inexperienced rider on a bucking bronco.

If we don't know how to manage our emotions, we are headed for serious trouble. I believe that psychology hasn't given us the proper answer to deal with the problem of uncontrolled emotions. It has basically just taught us how to cope and how to blame everyone else for how we feel and act so we don't have to experience guilt or take responsibility.

We can learn to control a horse, even though it is bigger than we are. But it can't be done through brute strength alone. There is a right way and wrong way to go about it, and it's the same with our emotions.

Psychologists are correct in the sense that we can't help but be hurt if someone hates us or mistreats us. In the natural, that's true. Emotions are such a strong force that when something negative happens to us on the outside, there is bound to be a negative reaction on the inside. That is physical truth; that's the way we are made. But with knowledge, we can learn to control those negative emotions. We can learn to manage them. We can harness them just as we harness a horse.

The Bit of the Bridle

Behold, we put bits in the horses' mouths, that they may obey us; and we turn about their whole body.

James 3:3

In the physical, I can't control a horse with my brute strength, but I can control a horse with my superior knowledge. When the Bible says that by putting a bit in a horse's mouth we turn about its whole body, it is referring to a physical, natural law. This is the way God made a horse. It can't do anything without its head leading it.

If a horse is lying down, you can sit on its head and hold that two-thousand-pound animal on the ground, because a horse cannot get up unless it physically throws up its head first. I don't know exactly why, but that's just the way it is. If you can hold a horse's head down, you can hold its whole body down.

Say you are riding a horse that has a tendency to get down on the ground and roll. You don't have to worry about that happening while you are in the saddle, because the horse has to dip its head before it can go down to its knees and roll over. If you hold that horse's head up, it can't get down. It might fall, but it's not going to get down as long as you hold its head up.

A horse cannot rear up unless it first throws its head up. So if you are riding a horse that tends to rear up, all you have to do is put a tie-down on it to keep its head from being thrown up.

If a horse tries to run away with you, you use the bit to rein it in. If the horse doesn't respond to the bit, all you have to do is pull the reins to one side. If you pull the reins to the right or to the left, you can stop the horse from running away with you. It is impossible for a horse to run straight ahead with its head turned back around toward the rider. It will simply start going into a circle and eventually stop. This is the simple way a bit works on a horse. If you can control a horse's head, you can control the entire horse.

The same is true with our emotions. Emotions are a powerful force in the natural, but that doesn't mean we have to be at their mercy. God intends for us to control our emotions. It is simply a matter of knowing God's truths from His Word and applying them to our lies.

God's Word is the bit, bridle, and reins that give us control over our emotions. When we live by God's Word, faith comes, and faith (knowing God) will override and neutralize any negative emotions. Then we can experience victory in our emotions.

That is exciting!

Chapter 3

The Mind and
the Emotions

As Christians, our sense of peace depends not on our outward circumstances but on our inward thoughts. If we think on the negative things of this world, we are going to be depressed because the things of this world are depressing. But if we think on the positive things of God, put our minds on heavenly things, and think about what God has given us, we are going to be blessed. It all depends on where we put our minds.

Where Is Your Mind?

Thou wilt keep him in perfect peace, whose mind
is stayed on thee: because he trusteth in thee.

Isaiah 26:3

If we really had our minds stayed on the awesome things God has done for us and has prepared for us, it would be impossible for us to be depressed and defeated, regardless of our present situation. There would be perfect peace.

Let not your heart be troubled: ye believe in
God, believe also in me.
In my Father's house are mansions: if it were
not so, I would have told you. I go to prepare a
place for you.

> **And if I go and prepare a place for you, I will come again, and receive you onto myself; that where I am, there ye may be also.**
>
> *John 14:1-3*

Jesus was saying, "Don't get all worried and upset. Just trust in Me. I have everything under control and am working it all out for you." That is also what Paul was talking about when He wrote the following scriptures:

> **But as it is written, Eye hath not seen, nor ear heard, neither have entered into the heart of man, the things which God hath prepared for them that love him.**
>
> *1 Corinthians 2:9*

> **For I reckon that the sufferings of this present time are not worthy to be compared with the glory which shall be revealed in us.**
>
> *Romans 8:18*

One of the reasons the Lord told us about the future and of the glories He has planned for us is because when we are in the middle of negative circumstances, we can close our eyes and think on these things (Phil. 4:8). We can think about our glorious future. We can think about the fact that this physical life is like a brief millisecond compared to eternity. And as we begin to think on these things, it will bring emotional peace and joy to us. We will find our peace in who we are in Christ and in what He's done for us, not in our physical circumstances.

The Mind Controls the Emotions

Your mind—the things you think about—control your emotions. If I were to tell you that one of your loved ones had been killed in a car wreck, there would be a physical, emotional response; there's no option. Even if what I told you was a total lie, you would still experience the emotions that go along with how you *think* about what I said. If you believed me, there would most likely be a reaction of grief, sorrow, or maybe even anger at God for letting such a horrible thing happen. If you knew I was lying, you would be angry with me, wondering why I would tell you such a thing.

I could tell ten different people the exact same thing, and their emotional reactions would vary, depending on how they perceived what I said to them. Some may believe me, some may not. But they have all, in some way, preprogrammed themselves to respond a certain way.

For example, a man who was totally selfish and really didn't love anyone but himself would respond differently from someone who was completely unselfish. If I told a woman who was 100 percent selfish that her husband had just died in a car wreck, she might thing, *Well, what about me? What's going to happen to me? How am I going to pay the bills without him?* A woman who was really in love with her mate would think, *Oh, I loved him so much! How am I going to live without him? I'm going to miss him terribly.*

There would be different reactions to the same piece of news because we are emotionally different. We think differently and emotions follow thought. So if we begin controlling the way we think based on the Word of God, then we can begin controlling the way we feel.

For example, we can learn to control our emotion of anger by looking at things differently. I have learned that when people are angry at me, it is not physical flesh and blood I am fighting, but demonic spirits (Eph. 6:12). Satan uses people to get to me. So when someone attacks me, I realize that it is really Satan who is attacking me and not that person. That understanding has helped me tremendously.

I have also realized that what really makes me angry is pride, my own self-centeredness (Prov. 13:10). If I weren't so concerned about promoting myself and if I loved other people more than I love myself, then I wouldn't have such a problem with my emotions. When someone gets angry and then violent, I think, *God, what's wrong with them? Why are they like that? What is causing them to be this way?* It's only a very selfish person who gets so angry that they become emotionally upset.

Now, you may say, "But it's hard not to get angry when people hurt you." That's true. But if we can diffuse that *self* on the inside of us, we can diffuse our anger. As we begin learning these keys through God's Word, it changes the way we think and ultimately changes our reactions. It changes us in the emotional realm. We don't have to go around like a bomb waiting to go off if certain things do or do not happen.

The Limit of Faith

Today many Spirit-filled Christians who have heard teachings on faith and how it can change their lives find themselves in situations where it just doesn't seem to work. They try to use their faith to rebuke the devil, to remove every obstacle in their paths, or to get to the place where no one will ever cross them or rub them the wrong way. They try to use their faith to get rid of all financial problems, all physical problems, and all emotional problems. Through faith, they try to change their external environment so they never have an occasion to get hurt. That is the goal some Christians have set for themselves, and I believe that to a degree, they can affect it.

For example, I believe God has provided financial prosperity for us. He doesn't want us to be financially destitute—He wants us to be prosperous (3 John 2). In the area of physical healing, I believe God has given us the authority to walk in divine health by faith. But I also believe that even if we had our faith working 100 percent of the time in those two areas, which doesn't happen overnight, we would still have problems to deal with. I'm not sure anyone ever gets to the place where they can never be touched in these areas. But even if they did—if they had their finances and their health in perfect condition—they would soon discover that there are other areas they do not have complete control over, such as other people and their wills.

We cannot manipulate and control human relationships with our faith. Whether we like it or not, other people always have a choice. We can influence them through our prayers and through our actions, but ultimately other people decide for themselves how they will think and act. Satan has more than enough people around who are submissive to him that he is always going to have someone he can parade across our paths, someone we cannot control, and someone who knows how to hit our "hot buttons."

The point is, if we are using our faith just to try to change our environment or our outside circumstances to where we have no problems, we will be sadly disappointed. It will never work. Never in a million years will we work up enough faith to have things our way, because there are always going to be people we can't control. As long as we are living in this world, we are going to be rubbed the wrong way—someone or something is going to bother us. The devil will see to that!

We are not to change our outward circumstances; we are to change our inner selves. We must change our emotions, our programming, and our attitudes so that regardless of what people do to us, we are going to walk in love. We are not going to be bummed out, and we are not going to have a bad day, no matter how other people treat us.

Decide to Rejoice

Although the fig tree shall not blossom, neither shall fruit be in the vines; the labour of the olive shall fail, and the fields shall yield no meat; the flock shall be cut off from the fold, and there shall be no herd in the stalls:

Yet I will rejoice in the LORD, I will joy in the God of my salvation.

Habakkuk 3:17-18

Some people cannot relate to this passage about rejoicing in the Lord regardless of their outward circumstances. They say, "Do you mean we can have peace no matter what is going on around us? Is it possible that our emotions can be totally disconnected from our environment to where they don't dictate to us the way we should feel?" Yes, that is exactly what I mean.

God is our refuge and strength, a very present help in trouble.

Therefore will not we fear, though the earth be removed, and though the mountains be carried into the midst of the sea;

Though the waters thereof roar and be troubled, though the mountains shake with the swelling thereof.

Psalm 46:1-3

This sounds like a major calamity, yet David did not fear. He rejoiced in the Lord. **"I will bless the LORD at** *all* **times: his praise shall continually be in my mouth"** (Ps. 4:1, emphasis mine). There are many instances of David praising and worshiping the Lord in the midst of his hardships. In spite of everything that was going on around him, he chose to worship God. He was confident that even if the earth fell apart, God was his refuge and his strength, and He would see him through.

We can *choose* to be joyful in the midst of negative circumstances *if* we will put our minds on what God says and focus our attention on the spiritual realm rather than the physical realm.

This hits at the very heart of what causes so many negative emotions, even in Christians today. With all the communications technology our modern society has available today, we are plugged into the world more than any group of Christians who have ever lived. We are bombarded with events and situations from around the globe: wars, natural disasters, plagues, epidemics, hunger, famine, and tragedies of all kinds. We have developed a global perspective, and much of it is negative because that is what most often attracts media attention. If we think on these negative things, sooner or later we are going to become negative. If we focus our attention on depressing things, we are going to become depressed. That's just the way it is.

Christians today have to make a deliberate decision not to allow these negative things to mold their thinking or determine their destinies. They have to constantly remind themselves that even though they are in the world, they are not of the world (John 17:11 and 16).

That doesn't mean God wants us to move into a monastery, bury our heads in the sand, and try to never hear anything negative again. But it does mean we have to make a deliberate effort to avoid becoming infected by the negative thinking that is so prevalent in the world today. It takes extra effort on our part to counter the negative things we continually hear and experience. We do that by going to the Word of God. We must let God's Word mold our thinking, rather than what we hear from the world.

> **My son, if thou wilt receive my words, and**
> **hide my commandments with thee;**
> **So that thou incline thine ear unto wisdom,**
> **and apply thine heart to understanding;**

> Yea, if thou criest after knowledge, and liftest up thy voice for understanding;
>
> If thou seekest her as silver, and searchest for her as for hid treasures;
>
> Then shalt thou understand the fear of the LORD, and find the knowledge of God.
>
> For the LORD giveth wisdom: out of his mouth cometh knowledge and understanding.
>
> *Proverbs 2:1-6*

> My son, forget not my law; but let thine heart keep my commandments:
>
> For length of days, and long life, and peace, shall they add to thee.
>
> *Proverbs 3:1-2*

The Word of God is super positive. There is an antidote in it for every negative thing we will ever hear or experience. Nothing will ever come our way that God's Word does not answer. So we must commit ourselves to the Word by reading it, putting it into our hearts, and meditating on it. God's Word will rise up with an answer to everything Satan throws against us.

The World's Way or God's Way?

You have a choice: Are you going to see things from the world's perspective or from God's perspective?

> And we know that all things work together for good to them that love God, to them who are the called according to his purpose.
>
> *Romans 8:28*

According to this scripture, God can make all things work together for our good. I believe that because I have seen it happen in my own life. I have things come against me just like everyone else does. Sometimes when I teach about overcoming emotions through faith in the Word of God, people will come up to me and say, "Well, brother, you just haven't had my problem." They discard what I say because they assume I haven't been in their exact situation.

I admit we are different and we all have different circumstances to deal with day by day, but the Bible says, **"There hath no temptation taken you but such as is common to man"** (1 Cor. 10:13). Satan does not have different tricks that he uses on different people; he has the same trick—he just puts it in a different package, uses a different wrapper, and adds a different bow to it. I have been through the same progression of temptations and have faced the same problems that plague everyone else, and I have seen faith in God's Word give me the victory.

One time we sent a letter to the partners of our ministry, asking them to help us prepay the printing of a Bible I had written. The total cost was $21,000. We received the money, and because we were naïve and stupid, we paid it all to the printer in advance to get a $10,000 discount on the printing fee. It turned out that the printer stole that money from us and didn't provide us a thing, so we lost all of the $21,000. That was a big hit for us. Besides that, to get the Bible reprinted, we had to come up with an additional $45,000 because that's what it normally took to get the job done. Our printer had bid low, knowing from the beginning that he was going to steal our money.

If you heard that you had just lost $21,000 and had to come up with an additional $45,000, how would you feel? What emotions would you have? Well, I guarantee you, I had a number of feelings and emotions. I was upset and hurt at the same time. I was embarrassed, thinking about our partners and the money they had given us in trust and knowing I had blown it. I had all kinds of negative emotions coming at me, but I also had the Word of God in my heart to counteract them.

We have seen that being spiritually minded produces life and peace. When these negative emotions came upon me, the first scripture that came to me was Proverbs 6:30-31, which say that if a thief steals something **"he shall restore sevenfold."** The Lord spoke to me and said, "That's nothing but the devil stealing from you and trying to hurt you, but he will have to repay seven times that amount."

I immediately grabbed hold of that word from the Lord. I called my staff together and told them, "This is going to be the best thing that has ever happened to us. It's the devil who stole from us, and we're going to rub his nose in it. We're going to get back seven times what we have lost.

I began thinking positively and focusing on the promise of God, and that turned our situation around totally. That year was the greatest financial increase we ever had to that point because I stood and believed God. I didn't go to my partners and ask them for more money; I just started believing God. We did some things on our own, but it was the blessing of God that caused that year to be the greatest financial year we had ever experienced. Our financial increase that year was nearly exactly seven times what the devil had stolen.

Now, some people may not see the miracle in that, but I guarantee you, it could have gone the exact opposite direction. That event could have totally shut us down. It could have ruined our whole ministry if I had conceived defeat through entertaining negative emotions.

When the Bible says in James 1:14 that lust, when it conceives, brings forth sin, we often think of sin as adultery, murder, robbery, and so forth. Those things are sins, but unbelief is also sin. Discouragement is sin. Depression is sin. Sin means to miss the mark. It's not what God intended for us. And the only way to counteract that sin is by standing on the Word of God in faith.

Thinking Spiritually

Unbelief, discouragement, and depression are conceived in the emotions. If we refuse to give place to self-pity, anger, bitterness and hurt, we won't conceive the failure these things breed.

In our problem with the printer, the Lord brought Proverbs 6:30-31 to my mind. Because of the Word of God, I started thinking spiritually, and God worked everything out to our good. He will do the same for anyone who keeps their mind stayed on Him rather than giving in to their negative emotions.

As we have seen, emotions are determined by thought. If you will start thinking in line with God's Word, He will show you a way to turn any negative thing in your life around so that it works together for your good.

I could give so many examples of people I have ministered to who have seen this principle at work in their lives. A certain single woman I know was raped and became pregnant. It was a terrible situation. She was so upset that she decided to get an abortion. But God spoke to her and said, "That's not your baby; she's Mine. You can't take her life." She turned her situation over to the Lord, and He began to show her that He could glorify Himself through it.

Now, that does not mean God caused her to be raped. No, it was an attack of the devil, but God turned it around for good. That woman has become healed emotionally. God has done many miracles in her life, and she is now seeing other people's lives changed through her testimony. In spite of her negative situation, God brought a positive result when she trusted in God and His Word instead of her emotions.

There's a positive way to think about everything. You may say, "But I'm going through a divorce. What's positive about that?" I'm not saying divorce is good, but you need to look at things in light of eternity. Recognize that this situation is just for a moment.

<u>Keeping Our Perspective</u>

Some time ago a woman came to me for counseling. She said, "I'm not a Christian like you and these other people around here, but I'm having marital problems. I'm going through a divorce. I need help, and I want you to pray for me."

"Now, wait a minute," I said. "You admit that you understand what being a Christian is, you know you aren't saved, and if you were to die you would go to hell?"

"Yes."

"But you want me to pray for you? You want to ask God for help in your marriage but not ask God for help in the salvation of your eternal soul?"

As she looked at me in silence, I went on to say, "You know, ten thousand years from now after you've been in hell for all that time, this marriage isn't going to be all that important. You're dealing with the most important thing in the world—the salvation of your soul—not your marriage."

All of a sudden the truth dawned on her. "Hey, you're right," she said. "I need to take care of my relationship with God." So I prayed for her, and she was born again.

Now, I'm not saying marriage isn't important! It is important. It is probably *the* most important decision you'll ever make concerning this physical life. And if you are facing divorce right now, I'm not saying you're not in a bad situation. But if all else fails, you can still say, "Father, some day this life will be over, and I will be with You for eternity. Thank You, God, that marriage is only temporary. This is all going to be behind me then. Thank You, Lord, for such a great salvation. Thank You that regardless of what the devil does to me here in this life, I still have You. Thank You that You love me,

You haven't rejected me, and that whatever happens to me, I am in Your hands now and forever."

As you begin thinking that way, do you know what will happen? You will begin experiencing joy and peace—not a peace you can find in the world, but a joy and peace only God can provide. And that peace will give you a fresh perspective and new wisdom about your problem.

What the Lord has given us through Jesus is greater than any problem we can ever experience here in this life. If we will take our attention off of our physical problems and begin to look at what God has done for us, we will experience joy and peace regardless of our physical circumstances.

As Christians, we have no excuse for being defeated. We can find many *reasons* why negative things happen to us, but there are no *excuses* for allowing those things to overcome us emotionally. Remember, God's provision is always greater than our need.

> **But my God shall supply all your need according to his riches in glory by Christ Jesus.**
> *Philippians 4:19*

The Outer Man and the Inner Man

> **For which cause we faint not; but though our outward man perish, yet the inward man is renewed day by day.**
> *2 Corinthians 4:16*

The Apostle Paul is giving us some background about himself. He is admitting that there are some serious things happening to him in the physical realm. One of these things is that his outward man is perishing—his body is getting older every day. But Paul is talking about more than just his physical body; he is also speaking of the spiritual realm in which the inward man is being constantly made new.

Paul is saying, "There is a physical world out there, and I am not denying that problems exist in it. But I am not being controlled by the physical realm. That is not what is dominating me. There is a spiritual me on the inside, and that's the part of me that contains the power of God. That's the part of me that is really alive. That's the part of me that I'm focusing on because it is eternal. It is not perishing, but I'm being renewed day by day."

If we are to overcome the emotions that assail us day after day, we must keep that distinction clearly in mind.

<u>Our Light Afflictions</u>

For our light affliction, which is but for a moment, worketh for us a far more exceeding and eternal weight of glory.
2 Corinthians 4:17

Paul didn't say this because he didn't have any problems; he had plenty! These were some of what he calls his "light afflictions":

I speak as concerning reproach, as though we had been weak. Howbeit whereinsoever any is bold, (I speak foolishly,) I am bold also.
Are they Hebrews? so am I. Are they Israelites? so am I. Are they the seed of Abraham? so am I.
Are they ministers of Christ? (I speak as a fool) I am more; in labours more abundant [I have worked harder than anyone else], **in stripes above measure** [I have been beaten with stripes so many times I can't even count them], **in prisons more frequent** [I have been put in prison more than

any other minister I know of], **in deaths oft** [I have been brought to the brink of death often, as in Acts 16, where I was stoned and left for dead].

Of the Jews five times received I forty stripes save one [on five different occasions I have received thirty-nine stripes].

Thrice was I beaten with rods [sticks large enough to break my bones], **once was I stoned, thrice I suffered shipwreck, a night and a day I have been in the deep;**

In journeyings often, in perils of waters, in perils of robbers, in perils of mine own countrymen, in perils by the heathen, in perils in the city, in perils in the wilderness, in perils in the sea, in perils among false brethren;

In weariness and painfulness, in watchings often, in hunger and thirst, in fastings often, in cold and nakedness.

2 Corinthians 11:21-27, brackets mine

Paul probably suffered more than most of us have ever thought about, yet he called it a **"light affliction."** That is awesome! How could he say that? It wasn't because he had fewer problems and hardships than we do, because he had many, many more. He considered these to be light afflictions because of his *perception* of those problems and hardships.

For I reckon that the sufferings of this present time are not worthy to be compared with the glory which shall be revealed in us.

Romans 8:18

Paul was so excited about the revelation of the Lord he had on the inside of him that all the things he suffered on the outside seemed like nothing in comparison. He didn't ignore the fact hat he had problems in this life; he just didn't focus on them. His "light afflictions" weren't just a moment in the light of this physical life.

He endured persecutions until the day he went to be with the Lord. But it was because of his attitude and the way he thought that he was able to keep things in perspective. He was able to look at his life in light of eternity, and in that light, his afflictions were just for a moment.

If we would learn to think that way, it would take a lot of the bite out of our problems.

A View of Eternity

When I was a child, I spake as a child, I understood as a child, I thought as a child: but when I became a man, I put away childish things.
1 Corinthians 13:11

Children don't have the benefit of the adult perspective.

When we were little, everything in our lives seemed so dramatic. If something happened that we didn't like, we thought the world had come to an end. Now that we are adults, we have a different perspective. We see that those things we once thought were so huge were actually minute in comparison to what life is really all about.

All of us can remember something from our childhood that seemed so traumatic, we weren't sure we would ever get over it. Now we look back and laugh, wondering how we could have been so immature. That is what Paul is talking about in these scriptures. When we get the perspective of eternity on the problems in our lives, it shrinks those problems down to where they become totally manageable.

I believe in healing. I know God wants us all healthy, but if a person is sick and never sees healing manifested in their earthly body, they can still have a positive outlook. Even if they are facing a miserable, horrible death, they can still experience joy and peace if they will focus their mind on eternity and the fact that because they know the Lord, they are soon going to be out of their body and with Him forever in glory—regardless of how traumatic that illness may seem at the moment. Probably every one of us can think of a scriptural example, or even an example from our own lives, of people who went out with a shout in the midst of terrible adversity because they had this view of eternity.

If you can't see anything physically uplifting around you, if there is nothing positive in your existence, if every time you look for the light at the end of the tunnel it turns out to be an oncoming train, and if there is nothing you can look to for hope and encouragement in this life, just close your eyes and think about eternity. Think about what God has done for you in the past and about what is going to happen to you when this is all over, and it will cause you to rejoice in the Lord.

Commanded to Rejoice

Rejoice in the Lord alway: and again I say, Rejoice.
Philippians 4:4

As you begin to look at your present circumstances in light of eternity, you'll quickly see there is no excuse for being discouraged, depressed, and despondent. There are reasons, but not excuses. God has given us so many great things in which we can always rejoice.

When Paul says to rejoice, it is a command, not an option. It doesn't say to rejoice if we *feel* like it, if we are in the mood, or if everything is going our way. I can say right now that most times, we won't feel like it. Most times we won't be in the mood. And most times things won't be going our way. However, we are still commanded to rejoice in the Lord at all times. God would not give us a command we could not fulfill. We can rejoice if we choose to do so, and He is showing us how we can do it.

Many people say, "But our music minister just doesn't play the right music. They don't sing the songs I like." Well, this scripture doesn't come with exceptions or conditions. They are to rejoice at all times. That means they are to rejoice in church, whether the minister plays the songs they like or not. They are to rejoice at home, whether their day is going great or not. They are to rejoice at work, whether they feel appreciated or not. They are to rejoice in the Lord at all times!

Look at it This Way

We look not at the things which are seen, but at the things which are not seen: for the things which are seen are temporal; but the things which are not seen are eternal.
2 Corinthians 4:18

Paul is saying, "I'm not dominated by what I see in the physical realm, because I'm looking at spiritual, eternal truth."

That's what we need to learn to do because there are always two sides to every issue in life. Whatever our problems, there is a physical side to them, and there is a spiritual side to them. How we deal with our problems depends upon which side we focus our attention.

I remember when interest rates went up to about 20 percent. Since I didn't own anything, it didn't affect me the way it did some. But many people were screaming about how bad the interest rates were. The media was reporting the failure of the economic system and how everything was falling apart.

I remember that in the midst of that situation, a prophecy came forth. The Lord said, "Yes, things look bad in the natural, but here's what's really happening behind the scenes. All this you're hearing is simply the wealth of the sinner being laid up for the just. All of the money that the world has been dominating is coming to the Christians."

The Lord began to bless Christian ministries—funneling millions and millions of dollars into the Gospel. And the Lord began to tell us, "There is more money going into the Gospel than ever before. Where do you think it is coming from? It is coming from the unbelievers. The world's system that has been dominated by unbelievers is falling apart, and the Christians are beginning to prosper."

That prophecy took us a step beyond the physical realm and let us see what was actually happening in the spiritual realm. It was exciting. People began to shout and praise God. They got their hope back and there was emotional peace, love, and joy. Why? Because they weren't looking at the things that were seen; they were looking at the things that were unseen. They were seeing that God was in control and that He was working everything for their good.

There have always been two sides to everything. If you look at things in the physical realm, you can get depressed. If I were to look at the potential problems in my life today, I could get as depressed as any person who is reading this book. I've had some really severe things come against me in the natural realm, but I can truthfully say that I have chosen not to be dominated by those things. I'm not ignoring them; I'm praying about them. I don't deny the fact that problems exist, but I refuse to focus on them. I refuse to be dominated by them. I am determined to rejoice in the God of my salvation. I don't care what the devil throws at me; he cannot come against me with anything greater than what God has already given me.

If the Lord never did another thing for me and if I suffered tragedy the rest of my life, I could still rejoice in what God has given me. That is a true statement—one that all of us should be able to make.

Refuse to look at the things that are seen, and look at the things that are not seen. Look at things that are eternal rather than temporal, and sooner or later, you will see those things manifested in your life. Believe it and rejoice in it because it's true!

Chapter 4

The Two-Fold Failure of Psychology

To a large degree, what I have said thus far in this book is borne out 100 percent by psychology today. Psychology comes to the same general conclusions as Christianity in that it tries to change people's emotions and actions by changing the way they think. Basically, the diagnosis I have made based on the Scriptures is shared by psychologists. But here is where I believe psychology and Christianity diverge.

I believe that while psychology may diagnose the situation properly, its solution is wanting at best, and at worst is potentially damaging. The reason I say that is because psychology actually leads people away from dependence upon God and into self-dependence.

Being humanistic, psychology views man as his own resource. It assumes that man is able to handle things that we Christians believe God never created us to take care of on our own. God did not intend for man to operate independently of Him and His supernatural ability.

Generally, psychology has rightly identified the problem, which for most people lies in their perceptions, their thoughts, and their attitudes. But there are two main areas in which I believe psychology fails to provide the proper solution to this problem.

The First Failure: Handling Guilt

First, psychology fails because of the way it tries to deal with the guilt that comes with the recognition that people's problems are caused by themselves. Psychology acknowledges that it is the way people think—the mental image they have of themselves on the inside—that becomes a self-fulfilling prophecy on the outside.

When a person comes to the point of recognizing they are responsible for their own problems, there is guilt associated with that recognition. Psychologists will admit that guilt is *the* dominant force behind most mental illness. It is one of the cardinal rules and practices of psychology to try to alleviate people of this sense of guilt.

I once heard a person talking on this subject who said that over 95 percent of all emotional problems are guilt-driven, meaning that guilt is the motivation behind the problems. So when a person goes to a psychologist for help, one of the very first things the psychologist does is try to absolve the patient of guilt. And the way psychology does that is completely different from the way God's Word does it.

What most psychologists do—specifically non-Christian psychologists and mental health experts who have no spiritual foundation whatsoever—is attack Christianity. Many view the Bible as the source of guilt and condemnation. It is the standard for what's right and wrong, and it prescribes punishment when a person falls short of that standard. Therefore, people are guilt-ridden because of Christianity, or Christian ideology. One of the very first things some psychologists will do with a new patient is take away their Bible and tell them Christianity is irrelevant, it's wrong, and its standards are inaccurate because everything in life is relative, not absolute. How very wrong they are.

The Purpose of Guilt

Now I rejoice, not that ye were made sorry, but that ye sorrowed to repentance: for ye were made sorry after a godly manner, that ye might receive damage by us in nothing.

For godly sorrow worketh repentance to salvation.

2 Corinthians 7:9-10

If a person is having emotional trauma because of homosexuality, many psychologists will say, "Who says homosexuality is wrong?" They will point to famous people who are homosexuals and try to show how well adjusted and successful these people are. They will try to change the rules or the standards set forth in the Bible by saying, "Homosexuality is not wrong." They will offer the patient excuses: "Don't you understand? This happened to you because you were abused as a child. You had a weak father figure, and that is what made you the way you are." Or they will resort to a non-condemning medical viewpoint: "You were born this way. It's in your genes. You can't help it." All of this is an attempt to remove the patient's guilt so their self-image will improve and any further damage caused by this guilt can be avoided.

I will agree that guilt is damaging. A person who lives under a prolonged sense of guilt is going to be miserable because guilt leads to depression and all kinds of mental and emotional problems.

If we can't see ourselves in a positive light, if we can't feel good about ourselves, if we hate ourselves and feel guilty, condemned, and filthy because of the things that have happened to us, naturally those negative things are going to affect our emotions and our actions. But the way to get rid of that guilt is not to change the rules, not to blame everyone else, and not to make excuses such as, "It's not my fault. It's just who I am. I'm a homosexual by nature." No, that's not right. There should be guilt associated with sin. It is true that over a prolonged period of time, guilt will kill. But for a brief period of time, it works for good.

Guilt is like the physical sensation of pain. If we touch something hot, it causes us to jerk back. In the same way, we should feel guilty when there is sin in our lives. That is what Paul was referring to in 2 Corinthians 7 when he spoke of godly sorrow for sin. If we go to the Lord and do what the Word of God prescribes, we can be forgiven of our sin and relieved of that burden of godly sorrow. We can take our sin to God and say, "Thank You, Lord, that through Your Son, Jesus Christ, I am forgiven. I repent of my sin and receive Your forgiveness and cleansing." That's the proper way to deal with guilt.

The good news is that once we repent and are forgiven of our sin, God never even remembers it. It's not something He is going to hold over our heads the rest of our lives. And the knowledge and acceptance of His divine forgiveness can set us free from guilt.

But psychologists as a whole do not bring God into the equation. Since many of them are humanists, they deal with things only from a human perspective. Therefore, they don't have the option of divine forgiveness. They don't have the blood of the Lord Jesus Christ to forgive and cleanse people, so they put the blame on someone else, telling the patient, "You aren't really responsible. You were sexually abused when you were a child. Therefore, you have no choice. You are going to be affected by it as long as you live."

What about Environment?

Many people say, "Well, isn't it true? Doesn't our environment mold us and make us who we are?" The answer is yes and no. Environment does have an influence upon us. It presents us with an opportunity, a crossroads, a choice. But whatever our environment or experiences, we can choose to become bitter or better. The choice ultimately lies with us.

I can prove this point to you. Take two women who have suffered identical traumas in their lives. Both of them have been sexually abused. Both were victims of incest when they were children. One woman allows the experience to literally destroy her life. It makes her hate and distrust men to the extent that it ruins her present marriage.

The other woman was abused just as much or even more, yet she chooses to turn to the Lord for forgiveness and cleansing, and she comes out of that experience a better person because of it. She has a compassion that allows her to minister to other people. There is literally no scar tissue and no negative effects in her life because of the experience. Through the blood of Jesus, only positive results come from the evil occurrences in her past.

In this example, both women came out of the exact same situation, and yet they got totally different results. Why? Because they made two different choices in the matter.

For another example, take two people who came from what psychology calls a dysfunctional family—one controlled by alcoholism and abuse. It's not uncommon to find that one of those family members becomes an alcoholic, while the other becomes a teetotaler— two exactly opposite reactions to the same negative situation.

I had an uncle who used to smoke. He finally saw the damage smoking did to other people, so he changed and went the exact opposite direction. He hated smoking to such a degree that if anyone smoked around him in a confined area, he would get sick and throw up. He was that way until the day he died, yet his brothers continued to smoke. They had totally different reactions to the same information because of the way they thought on the inside.

I believe our environment exerts a pressure upon us. It influences us a great deal. But ultimately, we have the choice over what we are going to do about it. Generally, psychology does not agree with that truth. It preaches that environment molds us 100 percent. Psychology often gives people excuses to stay as they are, because they are told it's not their fault. They think that is freedom, but it's not. It's bondage.

If circumstances rule our lives, then we really don't have much control in the matter. We are just helpless victims of our circumstances, and people who believe that live the rest of their lives as victims, not as victors. How can that possibly be freedom?

Old Victim or New Creation?

Therefore if any man be in Christ, he is a new creature: old things are passed away; behold, all things are become new.
2 Corinthians 5:17

In Charlotte, North Carolina, where I was ministering along these lines, a woman came up to me and told me she had been an alcoholic. Through Alcoholics Anonymous she had been dry for about two years. She wasn't on alcohol anymore, but she still had an alcoholic mentality. She was still a victim. She still felt the craving and the struggle on the inside of her every day of her life. She was not committing the physical action, but she was tormented in her emotions. She still saw herself as an alcoholic. She saw herself as a victim.

Programs like Alcoholics Anonymous reinforce a victim mentality in people. Every time these people go to a meeting, they stand up and say, "Hi, my name is so-and-so. I've been an alcoholic for X number of years, and I've been dry for X number of years."

They may be successfully resisting their craving for alcohol, but they still call themselves alcoholics. They still see themselves as victims who are simply coping, as contrasted with victors who have totally overcome. Through Christ, an alcoholic becomes a new person, a new creature, rather than merely an old victim just barely coping.

After I had talked about these very things, this woman came to me and said, "Through what you have been saying, I realize that in Christ, I am a new person, and I am not going to be victimized the rest of my life. Now I'm not only free from the action; I'm also free from the torment." That realization set her totally free. She had been blaming everyone else for her condition, thinking that because of her background, she had to adjust to her situation and live with those terrible emotions for the rest of her life. That's just not so.

Another area where modern medicine and psychology put people in bondage is what they call midlife crises. It is wrong to think that at age forty, because of a chemical response, it's time to have negative emotions. It's wrong to believe that you have to go through a midlife crisis.

Because psychology has become so prominent in our society today, people are actually looking forward to that time of their lives. They don't do it consciously, but nonetheless they make plans for failure. They expect certain problems to arise. They hear so much about the negative changes everyone is supposed to go through in life that when they experience some kind of physical or emotional reaction, they think, *Well, this is my midlife crisis*. They start giving in to it, letting themselves run the full gamut of emotions. Twenty-five years ago people were missing midlife crises because they didn't know they were supposed to have one. Today people are experiencing them, not because there's something physical that makes them have them, but because they have never learned to harness or control their emotions.

Psychologists have put fancy names on this phenomenon and have come up with all kinds of theories in an attempt to take away people's guilt and make them feel better. Today emotional complexes have become so popular that many people almost feel out of step with society if they haven't been through some kind of psychoanalysis and therapy.

For the believer, who is a new creation in Christ, their identity and security is found in Him. Instead of coping with alcoholism or a midlife crisis, they are set free.

Shifting the Blame

It really bothers me how psychology has shifted the blame for people's negative self-images. Today, if you don't blame your situation on the government, your race, or your social standing, you can always contribute it to your upbringing. Your family was dysfunctional; therefore, if you show any sign of emotional immaturity or insecurity, it's not your fault. You are just a victim of your environment. You were made the way you are.

I don't buy that.

I was raised in a loving family, but my dad died when I was twelve years old, so I grew up without a father. Psychologists today would say there's no way I could be normal. Surely I had to have experienced terrible trauma, rebellion, hurt, and all kinds of negative things. But that's not so. I never went through any trauma. I can honestly say that I never intentionally rebelled against my mother. I loved my mother to the degree that I never wanted to do anything to displease her.

"You know what's right and wrong," she would say. "You just do what you think you should." She never put a curfew on me, but the latest I ever stayed out at night was ten-thirty because I didn't want to worry her. I can think of only one exception when I came out of a show and found that I had accidentally locked my keys in the car. I had to ask the police to come open it up, but I called my mother and told her I was going to be late. I never lied to my mother. I never intentionally hurt her. I never went through the so-called "teenage rebellion."

Now, I did wrong sometimes because, like most kids, I was thoughtless and forgetful. There were times when my mother had to correct me. But even when I did wrong, it was not because of an attitude of rebellion.

However, according to current psychological thinking, because I grew up in a single-parent home, there is no way I could be normal. Maybe I'm not normal by today's standards, but I grew up without a lot of the problems I see people having today.

The point I am making is, if something negative happens in your life, you don't have to have a negative reaction. It is not predetermined. There is nothing physical that makes it that way. You can *choose* how you want to be.

Friends of mine have a daughter who just flipped out and went weird for a while. She got into drugs and other things and left home. It broke her parents' hearts. I talked to them about it often. Finally, the girl came back home. Her parents submitted her to Christian counseling that was more psychological than it was biblical.

The counselors began by telling her, "The reason this happened was probably because your parents didn't love you. They were too strict on you. They didn't allow you your own individuality. They were restrictive." They placed the blame for her actions on her parents.

Her parents are friends of mine, and I know they aren't perfect, because no one is perfect. We are human and we all fail. I am not saying these parents didn't do anything wrong, but they did give their daughter more than what 99.9 percent of others kids her age ever experience. They loved her and did their best for her. Maybe they did something wrong that someone can point a finger at, but there are literally millions of other kids who had it worse than this girl and didn't rebel. It irritates me that psychology put the blame on the parents, rather than on the daughter, who was responsible.

What would have set this girl free? Taking responsibility for her life by being accountable to God and honoring her parents.

The Blessing of Personal Responsibility

No doubt, there is plenty wrong in our lives! None of us are treated perfectly all the time, but that is no justification for us to act weird and then blame our behavior on our environment or upbringing. The truth is, we are responsible for our actions and our emotions.

You may be thinking, *But that puts people under guilt because it makes them feel personally responsible for their lives.* It's a blessing to face and accept personal responsibility. If everyone else is responsible for my feelings, then I'm in a world of trouble because I can't control everyone else. It's just a matter of time until someone comes across my path and ticks me off. It's a blessing, a release, and a step toward victory to find out that my problem is not what other people do to me; it's the way I respond because of my attitude.

A sense of personal responsibility causes us to ask, "Why am I responding like this to this person or situation?" Once we figure that out, we can begin to change.

We can't change everyone else, but we can change ourselves. We can change our thinking, which will change our emotions and our actions. Yes, responsibility may cause a bit of guilt and condemnation, but we can take that guilt and condemnation to the Lord. We can receive forgiveness and be released for it. That is the only real answer to this problem.

It is denial to blame everyone else and say, "It's my dysfunctional family that made me the way I am." No, they may have given you some real opportunities to mess up and they may have put pressure on you, but ultimately you are the one who chooses. Maybe it's because you didn't know the options. Maybe you hadn't really heard the Gospel. But you are the one who chooses how you are going to act and feel.

This escapism has happened since the beginning of time. In the Garden of Eden, when Adam disobeyed the Lord, God came to him and said, "Adam, what did you do?" Adam answered, "It's not my fault, Lord; it's that *woman* You gave me" (Gen. 3:8-12). Adam passed the buck to his wife. He blamed his actions and reactions on her. "Lord, it's what other people did that made me do wrong. Eve made me eat of this tree." But that wasn't true. Adam had a choice. Then he tried to put the blame on God. "Lord, if *You* hadn't given me this woman, this never would have happened."

People do the same thing today. "God, if *You* hadn't put me into this family, I would never have had these problems. God, if *You* hadn't given me this wife, or husband, or parents, I never would have ended up with these emotional scars."

It's not what other people have done to us that causes us to react the way we do—it's the way we think. It's that image we have on the inside of us that makes us act and react the way we do.

I believe the Bible differs dramatically with psychology in the assessment of who is responsible for our negative emotions. Psychology places the blame on everyone else. *The Bible holds us accountable for our own thoughts, words, and deeds because we have the power to control them. If that weren't so, God would be totally unjust to hold us responsible. Instead, He should judge everyone else for the things that take place in our lives.*

The Second Failure: Self-Dependence

The second failure of psychology is that it tries to improve a person's self-image by finding something positive they can focus on. I think a lot of Christians go along with that idea, thinking it is the right thing to do.

For instance, take the area of child training. Say your child is suffering rejections at school. The other kids don't like them because they may be overweight, ugly, or just different. So they develop a poor self-image. Their grades go down, and they show signs of depression. How to you respond to that situation?

Some Christian psychologists will say, "Find something positive about your child, something they can excel at, like sports. Find something they do well, and when they do well at it, praise them for it. Find something they can feel good about so they will develop a good self-image."

I understand that principle, and I agree that to a large degree, it works. Basically, that is the premise of all psychology. It tries to find something to make people feel good about themselves by focusing on one area of their lives in which they can succeed.

You are probably thinking, *Well, what's wrong with that?* I think the thing that's wrong with that is that regardless of what area people may succeed in, regardless of how they may prosper and do well in some area of endeavor, they are eventually going to fail. When they do, that failure will literally knock the props out from under them. It's okay to encourage your child in a sport they are good at. Children need your encouragement. But if their whole identity is wrapped up in their success at that sport, what is going to happen when they have an off day or lose a game? How are you going to tell someone to keep a stiff upper lip or improve their self-image when the very thing they put their confidence in is shaken?

Some people who have great talents or abilities in one area may be able to go for a long period of time having success. But that success is deceptive because it just makes them dependent upon themselves. Their joy, their emotions, their peace, their stability, and their self-image is dependent upon continual success, and that is not the way God made us to be. Our confidence and our self-image must be centered around God's Word.

The Danger of Self-Dependence

**Woe is me for my hurt! My wound is grievous:
but I said, Truly this is a grief, and I must bear it.**
Jeremiah 10:19

The prophet Jeremiah lamented over the terrible things that had happened to the nation of Israel. Known as "the weeping prophet," he grieved over Israel's punishment and the judgment God had brought upon them. He wept and travailed, crying out in anguish, "Lord it's so terrible what has happened to Your chosen people, the nation of Israel." But in the midst of his lamentation he began to justify and glorify God by saying, "Lord, You are just in bringing these terrible calamites upon us, because we rebelled against You and turned away from You."

Then Jeremiah makes this statement, **"O LORD, I know that the way of man is not in himself: it is not in man that walketh to direct his steps"** (Jer. 10:23).

Here he hits right at the very heart of one of the things that causes people not to accept God's direction—they become self-dependent. They get to thinking that *self* can do it. They become self-satisfied and self-sufficient. They begin to count on their own resources rather than entrusting themselves completely to God's will and wisdom, to His strength and ability.

When Jeremiah says that it is not in man to direct his own steps, he means that God did not create us with our own internal guidance system. He created us to depend upon His guidance so we can have His direction flowing through us. We are actually supposed to be remote-controlled by God.

The Lord made us so we could choose our own way. We have that choice. But the best choice a person can make is to say, "Father, I just don't trust myself. I am not self-dependent, self-reliant, or self-sufficient. I need You, Lord. Without You, I am nothing."

This thought is repeated many times in the New Testament. In John 15:5, Jesus said, **"Without me ye can do nothing."** In other words, "Without Me in your life, you're a big zero with the circle knocked off of it." That is the exact opposite of what psychology tells people, "Look, you're a great person. You need to feel good about yourself. Look what you can do." In Luke 9:23, Jesus went on to say, **"If any man will come after me, let him deny himself, and take up his cross daily, and follow me."** Here He was saying, "Unless you die to yourself, crucify yourself daily, and take up your cross and follow Me, you cannot be My disciple." Jesus taught self-denial.

So did Paul. In 1 Corinthians 15:31, he wrote, **"I die daily."** In Galatians 2:20, he went on to explain, **"I am crucified with Christ: nevertheless I live; yet not I, but Christ liveth in me: and the life which I now live in the flesh I live by the faith of the Son of God, who loved me, and gave himself for me."** Paul recognized that in himself, he was nothing. In Romans 7:18, he confessed, **"I know that in me (that is, in my flesh,) dwelleth no good thing."**

All of these scriptures are completely contrary to psychology. Psychology goes to great lengths to get people to feel good about themselves by developing a positive self-image. It builds on the foundation of self. It knows that if people feel guilty, filthy, unjust, and unworthy, than a negative self-image will reproduce itself in their inward emotions and outward actions. So psychology's answer is always to make excuses for all personal failures.

For example, it will tell a homosexual, "You didn't choose to be this way; you were born this way. It's your genes. You are this way because you were mistreated as a child, or you had a weak father figure." First, it places the blame on someone else. Second, it tries to get the person to feel better by saying, "It's not really wrong to be as you are. After all, it's just an alternate lifestyle."

This is actually the motivation behind the whole homosexual movement. Homosexuals are not asking for tolerance; they want approval to lift their self-esteem. It is based on the psychological principle of forcing society to accept homosexuals to a greater degree by stressing the fact that they should be free to be who they are. In other words, society has the problem, not the person who is gay.

So, in order to be "cool," society today basically allows a person to be homosexual. It does not bring judgment on them or any of the things they do. As a result, the homosexual is free to function openly, and woe to anyone who tries to discriminate against them.

They may be "out of the closet" in that sense, but they are fighting the emotional stress that goes along with being and doing something wrong. They are fighting guilt brought on by their sinful lifestyle. But rather than taking it to the Lord and asking for the forgiveness and cleansing God has to offer, they try to force society to go beyond simple tolerance, to acceptance. They want people to say, "There is nothing wrong with homosexuality. It is no longer a sin." That is why they fight so violently. It's not because they're being mistreated physically; it's because emotionally, they are trying to gain acceptance, thinking that will help them deal with their problem. And psychology is right there to support them by assuring them there is nothing wrong with them and that the fault lies with society.

Feeling Good or Facing God

Thou shalt not lie with mankind, as with womankind: it is an abomination.
Leviticus 18:22

According to the Bible, homosexuality is wrong. It is an abomination to God. The answer God gives to a homosexual is to become a new person in Christ.

Homosexuals don't need to feel good about themselves. Now that is a startling statement to some people, but it is true scripturally. Psychology's viewpoint is, "Any lifestyle you choose to follow is okay." I have even heard radio counselors make that statement to people who are into bestiality. There are basically no limits to some psychologists. To them, what people do with their bodies doesn't matter, as long as they feel good about it. But that's wrong. There are certain things people ought to feel rotten about.

When psychologists give a person that kind of counsel, it's not an answer to their problems. It's just like putting a Band-Aid on an amputated arm. It's not going to stop the bleeding, nor is it going to take away the pain.

> **For the wrath of God is revealed from heaven against all ungodliness and unrighteousness of men, who hold the truth in unrighteousness;**
> **Because that which may be known of God is manifest in them; for God hath shewed it unto them.**
> **For the invisible things of him from the creation of the world are clearly seen, being understood by the things that are made, even**

his eternal power and Godhead; so that they are without excuse.

Romans 1:18-20

Every person has an intuitive knowledge from God of what's right and wrong. Those who engage in sin numb themselves to it for the moment, but when they get quiet, they hear that still, small voice on the inside saying, "You're wrong; you're wrong." That may make them feel bad about themselves, but there is a positive benefit to it—it can lead to godly repentance, which leads to freedom.

Psychology tries to numb people to a conviction of right and wrong by doing away with standards, which is very detrimental. We are seeing that multiplied many times over in our society today. There are just not many standards of right and wrong left. Everything is negotiable—even the consequences to sin are negotiable—and that is damaging. It deadens people to the conviction of the Holy Spirit—though not completely—they still have that still, small voice on the inside. But as long as they are told that what they are doing is perfectly okay, they can feel justified and soothe their consciences.

But the Spirit explicitly says that in latter times, some will fall away from the faith, paying attention to deceitful spirits and doctrines of demons:

By means of the hypocrisy of liars seared in their own conscience as with a branding iron.

1 Timothy 4:2, NASB

Their consciences may be seared as with a hot iron, but that conviction still causes conflict within them. They instinctively know there is something wrong.

Denial of Right and Wrong

And he said to them all, If any man will come after me, let him deny himself, and take up his cross daily, and follow me.

For whosoever will save his life shall lose it: but whosoever will lose his life for my sake, the same shall save it.

Luke 9:23-24

One of the buzzwords psychology often uses is *denial.* If a person doesn't acknowledge personal emotional problems, psychologists will say that individual is in denial. But actually, psychology teaches denial. It teaches people to deny that there is a right and a wrong standard. Denial teaches them to refuse to confront their sins, because it has no forgiveness to offer them. There is no way psychology can bring people to a total reconciliation and an internal peace, because it does not recognize God's power to forgive. So psychology is actually in denial of the real problem—sin (who is to blame for it)—the person, and what the real solution to it is—forgiveness and deliverance through Jesus Christ.

As you have seen from the Scriptures, there is a benefit to feeling bad about your *self.* That's when you realize you can't do anything without the Lord. You need to know that. You need to know that, like Paul, in your flesh there is no good thing. You need to die to yourself. You need to get to where you hate your sin and the misery it ultimately causes you and those around you. Until you reach that point, you cannot be Jesus' disciple. That's not just what I say or even what Paul said; it's what Jesus said (Luke 9:23-24).

The Blessedness of Low Self-Esteem

For ye see your calling, brethren, how that not many wise men after the flesh, not many mighty, not many noble, are called:

> **But God hath chosen the foolish things of the world to confound the wise; and God hath chosen the weak things of the world to confound the things which are mighty;**
>
> **And base things of the world, and things which are despised, hath God chosen, yea, and things which are not, to bring to nought things that are:**
>
> **That no flesh should glory in his presence.**
>
> *1 Corinthians 1:26-29*

Most psychologists would blow up at the idea that people need to have a low opinion of themselves. "You're teaching people poor self-esteem," they would say. My answer is, "Look at what Paul said in the first chapter of 1 Corinthians."

Poor old Paul didn't have the benefit of modern-day psychology. He said that God deliberately chooses those who are not mighty or noble but the foolish, the weak, the despised, and the nothing in their own eyes. That is exactly opposite of what psychology teaches today. "How does this fit into the message of positive self-esteem?"

Keep in mind that the image, or the perception, we have of ourselves affects our actions and our emotions. We cannot operate differently from the way we think (Prov. 23:7). So how does this low self-esteem square with that concept?

Here the Bible teaches us that we need to see ourselves as nothing, as despised, and as incapable of doing things on our own. Why? Because it is not in the way of a man to direct his own steps (Jer. 10:23).

We must have a total distrust in ourselves. Yet if we feel that way, if that is the image we have of ourselves, how can we ever have good emotional health? The answer is that we have to quit trying to act like something we're not and instead actually become what we are—something brand new.

If you are suffering from low self-esteem, be encouraged! When Jesus comes into your life, you become a new person. This is the answer for the *Christian*, and only for the Christian. There is no way to obtain emotional health without a total transformation through the power of God.

So the two-fold failure of psychology is first to deny guilt and second to find a person's source in self instead of God. This perpetuates the lie that there is no God to be accountable to, which means there are not absolutes of right and wrong to feel guilty about. Their "sin" becomes "a problem," which is solved by positive thinking and shifting blame to others. God, on the other hand, wipes sin out through the blood of Jesus Christ when you acknowledge your sin as sin, turn from it, and ask Him to forgive you and cleanse you. When your source is God and not yourself, you can be free from sin and enjoy the life of blessing God has for you.

Chapter 5

A New Person

Therefore if any man be in Christ, he is a new creature: old things are passed away; behold, all things are become new.

2 Corinthians 5:17

God does not intend for a rebellious, sinful person to feel good and have great emotional health. If you are not living a life submitted to God and under His control and power, you are not going to feel good about yourself. You *should* feel bad. Hopefully, your feelings will drive you to the place of saying, "God, I need You. Forgive me. Come into my life and save me from sin and death."

The Lord is the answer, and the way to receive that answer is by coming to Him through His Son Jesus and becoming a new person in Christ.

Psychology is doing a tremendous amount of damage by prescribing us to cope without God. We aren't supposed to cope without God. God is the answer for our emotions. There is no pill that can ever mean to us what God means to us. If we can take a pill to numb ourselves and get rid of our depression and discouragement, something's wrong. We either need to get our bodies healed or our thinking straight.

God never intended for a pill to do what the Gos-pill was designed to do!

The Two Men

Put off concerning the former conversation the old man, which is corrupt according to the deceitful lusts;

And be renewed in the spirit of your mind;

And that ye put on the new man, which after God is created in righteousness and true holiness.

Ephesians 4:22-24

If you are a Christian, you have become a totally brand-new person. Now, that doesn't mean your old *person* ceases to exist; it means your old *nature* ceases to exist. You are no longer, by nature, a child of the devil, but all of your old feelings, your old emotions, and your old perceptions about yourself are still in your mind. Your new spirit is the new man within you who is different from your old man.

When we are born again, we still have this old part of us that was controlled by wrong attitudes. The Bible calls that old part the "old man." But we also have a brand-new person on the inside. That's what the Bible calls our "new man."

That very simple terminology is used in many different places in Scripture. We have already read Ephesians 4:23, which tells us to be renewed in the spirit of our minds. The verse before it says that we should put off the "old man." Then the next verse after it says that we are to put on the "new man," which is created in righteousness and true holiness. So right there in just three verses, the Bible uses the terminology "old man," referring to everything negative about us before we were born again, and "new man," referring to who we have become in Christ. It shows that there are now two different personalities on the inside of us.

Here is the answer to our apparent problem. I said earlier that the way we view ourselves—our mental image we have on the inside—determines our actions and our emotions on the outside. Yet the Bible teaches us that we need to see ourselves as nothing in order for God to use us. So if that is the image we have of ourselves, how can we ever have emotional joy and peace? We can have those things because within each of us, there is a new person in Christ.

If you are a Christian, you are a new person in Christ, and that's something to feel good about. But you still have this other self, this old self, this old man within you that is base, despised, weak, and nothing. You need to recognize that in that old self, you don't have the power to govern your life. You aren't smart enough to make the best choices. You need to disdain that and die to it. You need to constantly reject your old selfish attitudes, feelings, and emotions to find your new identity in Christ.

There are actually two yous: the new, born-again you and the old, unregenerate you—the new man and the old man. You should feel good about the new man. As you begin to see who you are in Christ, that revelation should give you joy, peace, confidence, and security. But at the same time, you must recognize that the old man is not godly and cannot be trusted. It should not be propped up and improved.

Few people have a real mental picture, image, or revelation of who they are in Christ. Most of us continue to think about ourselves in the emotional or mental realm, which the Bible calls the soulish part of us. Most of us think that is the real us, but it's not.

The truth is, there's a new you on the inside, and you've got to get into God's Word and find out who you are in Christ. Then you can begin to feel good about that new part of yourself. That's the part of you that is saved. That's the only part of you that is worth thinking good about.

Psychology doesn't have this option. Most psychologists don't believe that anyone can become a new person. They would ridicule this idea, saying, "What you're talking about is a dual personality. That's schizophrenic!"

A Dual Personality

Although I don't have the clinical terminology to debate with psychologists on this subject, I will agree with them on one point. Yes, I do have a dual personality. There is a born-again me, and there is a part of me that is not born again, is corrupt, and has wrong thoughts and attitudes. I'm not going to get better in that area, so there's no point in trying to improve it.

Many people have a wrong understanding about salvation. They don't understand that when they are saved, there is a part of them that is completely new, a part that is holy and pure and no longer subject to corruption. Instead, they think salvation is simply bringing their old self to the Lord, confessing that they have sinned, and letting God forgive them, cleanse them, and point them in the right direction, saying, "Now, go and do it right this time." They think salvation is like a new beginning or a new start with the same old self living within them.

That is a terrible concept of salvation! Furthermore, it's incorrect.

If all God did was forgive me of my past sins, pick me up, dust me off, and kind of point me in the right direction without changing me on the inside, then I would be bound to fail again. I would blow my second chance just as I did my first chance. That's not salvation; that's misery.

Yet that's the way many Christians see salvation. I know people who honestly made a commitment to the Lord and are born again, but they don't understand it properly. They're out there on their own, trying to live for God in their own energy and ability, trying to live a good life instead of a bad life, just as they were doing before they were saved. And they're winding up frustrated to the max.

They actually think they can live for the Lord in the flesh, which is another Bible term for the old man. Some people think that the fleshly part of them is actually going to get better and better as they continue to walk with the Lord. They see themselves improving in their flesh, when the Bible teaches that the flesh never improves. It teaches that the flesh is still the old personality with all of the desires and emotions that go with it.

Actually, as Christians mature they should get to where they depend less and less on the flesh, deny the flesh more and more, and let this new person they have become in Christ live through them. As Paul said in Galatians 2:20, "I am crucified with Christ. I live, yet it's not me. I'm alive, but it's not really me. It's not that old me. It's not the part I used to consider me. It's not the old man but the new man—the one in whom Christ lives. So the life I now live, I live by the faith of the Son of God, who loved me and gave Himself for me."

Christ in You

God would make known what is the riches of the glory of this mystery among the Gentiles; which is Christ in you, the hope of glory.
Colossians 1:27

Paul had a revelation of who he was in Christ. He recognized that there was a new man living within him. He knew it wasn't him living for God, but it was God living through him. He knew there was a new Paul that was in union with Christ, which he literally called "Christ in him." Because that union was so strong, he could refer to the born-again part of him and say, "It's not me; it's Christ living through me."

That's the attitude every Christian ought to have. When some people are first born again, they see themselves as weak and totally dependent upon God. But as they grow in the Lord, they actually think they should become more independent. They think they should be strong enough that they don't have to call upon God and ask Him for help. They think they should be so spiritually mature that they are able to do everything for themselves. That's a totally wrong concept.

The truth is, as we grow in the Lord, we ought to become more and more aware of our weaknesses and our frailties in the old man and more and more dependent upon the new, born-again life God has placed on the inside of us.

If you don't understand this truth, you will actually become dependent upon *self*, which is basically the same attitude psychology has today. That's the reasoning behind all the self-help groups, which are so popular that even churches are organizing them. That whole concept flies in the face of true Christianity. Self can't really help self. All self can help is someone else who is totally destitute and has no one else to turn to whatsoever. A self-help group may help you help someone who is living in the gutter, but compared to what God intends for you, self cannot help you.

Imagine yourself standing in a mud puddle trying to get your feet clean. You lift one foot up and clean it off, but then to raise the other foot, you have to stick the clean one back down in the mud. It's an endless process and a frustrating, unobtainable goal to try to get both feet clean that way. Yet that is exactly the way self-help groups work. They may help you to a degree. You may get dry from alcohol, for example, but you aren't going to get *delivered* from it.

"I'm an Alcoholic"

One time I was on a television program with a very famous actress. She had become an alcoholic, gone through a treatment center, got dried out, and was now talking about her deliverance. It sounded good on camera, but I was with her and her husband for two days behind the scenes. I can tell you that that woman was still addicted; she just wasn't addicted to alcohol. She didn't drink alcohol anymore, but she had to have cases of caffeine-free diet Dr. Pepper around at all times. There was never a waking moment when she was without a glass of Dr. Pepper in her hand.

This woman was no longer an alcoholic, but she still had the mentality of an alcoholic. She was still an addict. She talked constantly about the struggle she was going through. She was a victim. She was never delivered. She didn't know who she was in Christ, yet there she was on a Christian television network saying she was a Christian.

Behind the scenes, I talked to her and her husband, who was a fanatical born-again Christian. He truly loved God, and we had a great time together. But in private, this woman would say, "You know, my salvation experience was getting dried out in the treatment center. My husband talks about being born again, but I've never had that happen to me."

Yet there she was portraying herself as a Christian. I believe all she did was get some self-help, and the Christian host couldn't distinguish between that and genuine salvation. She was no longer on the bottle, but she was still addicted emotionally. She wasn't free, because she still had the same old spirit ruling and reigning within her.

A New Spirit

Many Christians don't really understand what it means to be born again. The true salvation experience is where you come to the Lord with nothing in yourself to depend upon. You aren't trying to clean yourself up; you ask God to do it for you. You cry out, "God, save me." Then the Lord saves you, but not by just winding your old self up and giving you a new start. If He did that, you would never make it. Instead, He takes away that old, dead spirit on the inside of you—the old spirit that corrupted your old man and taught it to hate and do all kinds of sinful things—then puts within you a brand-new spirit, one that is exactly as He is.

If you have received the Spirit of God, then you have His life, His nature, and His ability on the inside of you. From the time you receive Jesus Christ and the Holy Spirit comes to live in your new holy spirit, you have the ability to live the Christian life as a new creature. You should see yourself as a new person in Christ and begin to let that new person rule and reign.

If you don't have a good mental picture of yourself as a new person in Christ, you will continue to operate the way you used to before you were saved. That is what many Christians do. Lots of people come to the Lord and are genuinely born again, but because they don't know who they are in Christ, they continue to operate on the old information that was given to them. It's like a computer: it's going to continue to function under the programming that's in it until it's reprogrammed.

Reprogramming Your Old Mind

When you are born again, you need to get rid of the old information. You need to reprogram yourself by seeing yourself as a brand-new person in Christ.

I once heard Kenneth Hagin say that before he was born again, if he ever had a natural talent, it was the ability to pick a lock. He never saw a lock he couldn't pick. Because of his ability, if the people he ran with wanted to break in and steal something, they would always get him to pick the lock and let them in.

Right after he was born again, some of his friends asked him to pick a lock so they could go in some place and steal something. Brother Hagin said that he didn't understand everything about the Christian life, but one revelation he had was 2 Corinthians 5:17, which told him he was a new creature. He knew he was a different person. He wasn't looking at himself with that same old image anymore. He didn't have the old mental picture of himself as a person who picked locks. He now saw himself as a new being, created in the image of God.

So he told his friends, "I can't do it."

"Why not? they asked.

"Because I'm a new person."

I'm sure he didn't know exactly how to explain it to them, and it probably didn't register with them. But the point is, he had switched images on the inside. He saw that he was a different person. *He no longer saw himself as a thief, so he couldn't be a thief.*

See Yourself as Jesus Sees You

Strip yourselves of your former nature [put off and discard your old unrenewed self] which characterized your previous manner of life and becomes corrupt through lusts and desires that spring from delusion;

And be constantly renewed in the spirit of your mind [having a fresh mental and spiritual attitude],

And put on the new nature (the regenerate self) created in God's image, (Godlike) in true righteousness and holiness.

Ephesians 4:22-24, AMP

You can't be a thief if you don't see yourself as a thief. You can't commit adultery if you don't see yourself as an adulterer. You can't be a liar if you don't see yourself as a liar.

If we were really able to see who we are in Christ, we could see how holy and pure we have become through Jesus. Then this new image of ourselves would be reflected in our emotions and in our actions. That is powerful!

Imagine a woman who was a prostitute before she was born again. Suppose she really asked the Lord to save her. She truly put her faith in Him and believed she was forgiven. But imagine that she didn't change her image of herself. If she saw herself as just a forgiven prostitute, eventually she would go back into prostitution, or at least into a promiscuous lifestyle. Why? Because it would be impossible for her to consistently operate differently from the way she saw herself.

On the other hand, suppose that same woman was not only born again, but she renewed her mind. Suppose she could see herself as a new person—righteous, holy, pure, and clean. If she could get a vision of that, I guarantee you, it would be reflected in her life. She would no longer stoop to that old lifestyle, because she would not want to take the great gift God had given her and put it back into that kind of situation.

Christians are failing in the area of controlling their actions and emotions because they don't know who they are in Christ. They are looking at their physical circumstances and listening to what others are saying about their old person. They aren't listening to what God says about that new, born-again part of them. They see themselves as failures, and it becomes a self-fulfilling prophecy. Psychology and our society call this a lack of self-esteem.

Self-Esteem or Christ-Esteem?

I agree that the area of self-image and self-esteem is critical, but it all comes down to which *self* is being esteemed. It is not our old, carnal self but our new, born-again self that we need to focus on and esteem.

It's not really accurate for Christians to use the term *self-esteem*. It would be more accurate for us to say "Christ-esteem." As Christians, we are not to esteem our old, fleshly, carnal selves; rather, we are to esteem our new, born-again selves. When we do that, not only will our actions and our emotions be affected, but when we blow it, we won't be surprised and discouraged. We will recognize that the old fleshly part of us, which has never been saved, has been allowed to rule. It's not going to be saved, but it is eventually going to be replaced.

Our spirits are already brand new, but our soulish part and our physical bodies have not been saved yet. They have been purchased—salvation was purchased for them at the cross—but it's not a reality yet. Our physical bodies have to change, and our souls have to change. Our spirits are the only part of us that are completely saved.

Our soulish man is not saved, and it's not getting better. It's corrupt and it's never going to be any better until we go to be with the Lord or until He comes back for us. If we understand that truth, then when we have negative feelings and emotions, instead of being shocked or thinking *How could I think such a thing*, we will realize, *Oh, that's just my old flesh, because my new man doesn't think that way.*

When we esteem our new man, we focus on Jesus and esteem Christ in us. This makes us aware that we are brand-new spirits. And when we keep ourselves spiritually minded, we can more easily walk according to the spirit and not the flesh. If a person isn't very conscious of who they are spiritually, it's easy for them to slip back into the physical. Let me give you an example.

I had a friend who loved the Lord. He had been the pastor of a church and is a great man of God whom I really appreciate, but he went through some hard times. He was out of work for over a year, and his physical circumstances were negative. He began thinking and entertaining emotions that he should never have thought and entertained. He got to thinking that he wasn't providing for the family, so he got down on himself. He was looking at things in the natural—seeing himself as a failure rather than seeing himself in Christ. Because of that, in a moment of weakness, he got angry at God, threw his Bible out the window, and actually took an overdose of drugs, which is what he used to do before he was born again. As a result, he wound up in the mental ward of a hospital.

I went to visit this man with my associate minister. By the time we visited him, he had come down off the drugs and was aware of the mess he had made of things. When we walked in, he really didn't want to see us. He was so embarrassed that he didn't want to talk to us. It was a terrible sight to see. He just kept saying over and over, "I can't believe I did this. I thought I was more mature than this. I thought I was beyond this. How could a person who has loved God, witnessed for Him, and been a pastor do something like this?"

Basically, the way we ministered to him was by pointing out to him, "It's your spirit man that is complete. It's that born-again part of you that has the ability and the life of God. Your flesh is not capable of living a Christian life. Instead, it is capable of anything you were ever capable of. All that happened was that *you quit operating by who you are in Christ and instead went back into that old man. Instead of esteeming Christ in you, you esteemed your self and you failed.* That doesn't mean you have lost a thing. You still retain your righteous position with the Lord. You are still the same person spiritually. All you have to do is *step back into the spirit.*"

It's like flying an airplane. Because of the plane, you are able to do things beyond your physical ability. You are able to fly. You are able to reach altitudes and speeds you could never reach on your own. But you must remember that it is your union with that plane that makes it all possible. The moment you get back into your self and step out of a flying plane, you will fall to the earth like you always would have.

Likewise, it is only our union with Jesus Christ through our new born-again spirits that gives us power to overcome. When we step back into our old self, we are destined to experience the same problems we had before.

That is so simple, yet most people don't grasp this concept. They don't understand this new self—the born-again self. They try to improve the carnal self, and when they fail, hopelessness sets in. They have to go back to ground zero and start over.

God is not out to improve your carnal man; he wants you to deny it, turn from it, recognize that it's a mess, and realize that it's not getting any better. Retreat from it and go back into the spirit. Become the new person you are in Christ.

<u>Whose Thought Is That?</u>

Lest Satan should get an advantage of us: for we are not ignorant of his devices.
2 Corinthians 2:11

Satan tries to keep Christians ignorant of who they are in Christ by deceiving them in the realm of their thoughts.

For example, instead of coming to a man and announcing "I'm the devil. Look at that woman over there. Don't you think she is beautiful? Wouldn't you like to…?" he places a thought in the man's mind: *I like that woman over there. She's beautiful. I really would like to...* The devil doesn't come in the form of a demon on the outside; he comes in the form of thoughts on the inside. And most Christians aren't smart enough to figure out, "Hey, this isn't my thought. This is the devil's thought. That's not me thinking these things. It's Satan."

One of the first times I became aware of this fact was not long after my wife and I were married. We were at my in-laws' house for the holidays, and they asked me to say the blessing over the food. As I started to pray, a terrible, blasphemous thought against the Lord came to my mind. I couldn't believe I was thinking such a thing. I didn't say anything to anyone, of course, but for days I prayed about it. "Lord, what did I do to bring on such a thought?" Finally, the Lord showed me that it wasn't my thought, that I had never thought that way in my life. It wasn't me; it was the devil who spoke that thought to me. But he spoke it in the first person and made me think it was my thought.

How do you determine if it's the devil who's putting thoughts, attitudes, and images on the inside of you? How do you know whether it's the devil or God? How do you know if it's your old man or your new man? There is a very simple answer: You go to the Word of God, which tells you exactly what your new man is like—how your spirit thinks, feels, and acts.

For the word of God is quick, and powerful, and sharper than any two-edged sword, piercing even to the dividing asunder of soul and spirit, and of the joints and marrow, and it is a discerner of the thoughts and intents of the heart.

Hebrews 4:12

The Word of God is alive. It is the only thing that can be 100 percent accurate in dividing between what is your spirit—that new, born-again you—and your soul—the old, unregenerate part of you. It is the only thing that can discern between the thoughts and the intents of your heart. It is the only thing that can tell whether your thoughts are from God or from the devil.

If what you are thinking or feeling lines up with the Word, then that's the new, born-again you. If what you're thinking or feeling doesn't line up with the Word of God, it's the carnal part of you or the devil. If it's the carnal part of you or the devil, you simply reject that thought or emotion based on the Word of God.

Say, for instance, someone begins to criticize you, and you start to get so angry at the person that you're ready to let them have it. Suddenly, you stop and ask yourself, "Is it right or wrong?" You go to the Word of God, which says in Ephesians 4:32 that you are to **"be ye kind to one another, tenderhearted, forgiving one another, even as God for Christ's sake hath forgiven you."** In Galatians 5:22-23, you read that **"the fruit of the Spirit is love, joy, peace, longsuffering, gentleness, goodness, faith, meekness, temperance."** After reading these and other such scriptures, you see that you are to walk in love with all men, and you are to forgive even as God has forgiven you, meaning that you forgive even before you are asked to forgive.

As you listen to the Word, you say to yourself, "This emotion of anger toward this person is not the born-again me, because it doesn't line up with the Word of God. It's not my new self; it's the carnal part of me." So you say, "I refuse that thought. I reject it in the name of Jesus. I am going to love this person."

Always line your thoughts up with God's Word. Operating on this scriptural principle is part of letting the Holy Spirit rule and reign over your emotions and actions, and this can make a powerful difference in your life.

The Life of God

Some people misunderstand this principle of applying the Word of God to their lives and say, "What you're preaching is just mind over matter. You're saying that all we need to do is start thinking positively, and everything will be okay."

No, that's not what I'm saying. That's what humanists say. Humanists tell us that if we will all visualize world peace, it will come to pass. They tell us that if we think good thoughts, everything will be good. What they're missing is that a person who doesn't have the life and ability of God on the inside cannot produce life on the outside—no matter how hard they may try. It doesn't matter how we get our thinking straightened out; if there is nothing but death on the inside of us, all our minds can release is death. But if we've been born again, we have the life of God on the inside that is like a valve that opens the flow of God's life-giving Spirit.

Imagine the right side of yourself as being your spirit that is now born again with the life of God. Imagine the left side of yourself as the world, including your physical body and person. In the center is your mind, which is like a pipe or a valve. It can either be closed, blocking the flow of the spirit, or it can be open, allowing everything that is in the spirit to pass into the physical realm.

The mind is important. The way you think and the way you perceive yourself in the spiritual realm is going to determine what happens to you in the physical realm. But if you are a lost person, you don't have a new spirit. Because you aren't born again, the spirit that is within you is dead in trespasses and sins. It is by nature a child of the devil (Eph. 2:3). If your spirit has nothing but corruption in it, then no matter what you do with the valve of your mind, nothing but corruption can flow into the physical realm.

We could have the best faucet money could buy, but if we hooked it up to sewer lines, then whatever it was plumbed to would be what would come out. Likewise, our minds are like faucets that release or block what is in us. Only Christians who have the life of God on the inside of them can release life by the renewing of their minds.

Mind over matter may affect your feelings temporarily, but you can't really release life if there is no life on the inside. But if you're born again—if you have the life of God in you—then your mind is the critical factor. It is important how you think and how you perceive yourself. The image you have on the inside is going to determine whether your mind is closed and is operating out of your physical human ability or whether you release the life of God into the physical realm around you.

> **Not that I have already obtained all this, or have already been made perfect, but I press on to take hold of that for which Christ Jesus took hold of me.**
>
> *Philippians 3:12, NIV*

There are times when I experience great victory in the area of emotions, but I'm not perfect. I haven't arrived, but I have left! If a person gets mad at me, I am still tempted to feel bad. But when I feel depression, rejection, hurt, anger, bitterness, or any other negative emotion rising up in me, I know exactly why I feel that way. It's because of the flesh—the old me. Emotions just serve to warn me that the reason I am feeling that way is because I am living in the flesh. I say, "Father, forgive me. I'm a new person in You and in Christ. I'm going to start releasing Your love."

I take the valve of my mind and start opening it so I can allow the new person on the inside of me to start flowing out. I start thinking about love, joy, and peace. I start seeing that the same love that filled the mind and heart of Jesus has now been deposited on the inside of me. As I see Jesus loving the people who mocked Him and crucified Him, I start loving the people who are ridiculing me and saying bad things about me. As I think the way Jesus thought, the life of God that is in my spirit starts flowing right through my physical body. I begin to express it in my emotions and in my actions.

That's why it is so important for us to renew our minds and conform to the mind of Christ.

Renew Your Mind—Renew Your World

I beseech you therefore, brethren, by the mercies of God, that ye present your bodies a living sacrifice, holy, acceptable unto God, which is your reasonable service.

And be not conformed to this world: but be ye transformed by the renewing of your mind, that ye may prove what is that good, and acceptable, and perfect, will of God.

Romans 12:1-2

In our spirits, we have everything we need to live the victorious Christian life. So, what is stopping us from doing that? We haven't renewed our minds.

According to Romans 12:1, the first step in serving God is the giving of our entire lives to the Lord. But the second verse goes on to say that we are not to be conformed to this world. I like to say, "Don't be poured into the world's mold." So the next step is the renewing of the mind.

When we present ourselves as a sacrifice unto the Lord, He comes and lives on the inside of us, but the rest of our Christian lives are spent being transformed by the renewing of our minds. In the Greek, the word translated "transformed" in this verse is *metamorphoo*, which is the root of the word *metamorphosis* (James Strong's, *The Exhaustive Concordance of the Bible* [Nashville: Abingdon, 1890], "Greek Dictionary of the New Testament," #3339.) This is the process that takes place when a caterpillar spins a cocoon, lives in it, and is transformed into a butterfly.

To have that kind of transformation take place in your emotions and your actions, you must renew your mind. Go through the New Testament, and read and meditate on all the scriptures that describe who you are in Christ. Recognize that when you made Jesus Christ the Lord of your life, you were born *again*. You don't just get a new start or a new beginning; you have an entirely new life. There is a totally new person on the inside of you.

Then recognize that just as you were incapable of saving yourself, you are incapable of living the Christian life. It's not just hard; it's impossible for your old man to ever measure up to the new life. God had to give you a new man—a new person who is exactly as Jesus is, with His life, His nature, and His ability on the inside.

Get a mental picture of who you are in Christ. As you think in your heart, that's the way you are going to be. If you think of yourself as an old sinner saved by grace, that's how you'll be. If you think salvation wasn't a transformation but just a canceling of your past debt, you will continue to see yourself as a sinner. If you don't see yourself as a new person, but only a sinner saved by grace, you will wind up sinning again and again and never be an overcomer.

But if you can begin seeing yourself as a brand-new person in Christ, you will begin to emotionally feel and physically act the way you are in Christ. Your mindset will be reproduced in your lifestyle. The Word of God—how God describes you—will be your image of yourself.

Get a real revelation of that concept, and begin changing the way you think. Change the perception you have of yourself from the old nature to the new nature. You are today the way you see yourself to be (Prov. 23:7). If you are defeated, angry, bitter, depressed, or lonely, it's because you see yourself that way. You are seeing yourself in light of your problems. You are looking at failure and receiving what you see. But if you can begin to see who you are in Christ, then you can begin to reproduce that image in your actions and your emotions and find hope for today and tomorrow.

When you get saved, the Lord makes you a new person. If you have never made that commitment, I encourage you to do so today. Let the Lord make you a new person. Become born again by accepting His only Son Jesus Christ as your Savior and Lord. Receive His Holy Spirit to teach, guide, protect, and empower you. Then you can begin to esteem that new self we have talked about, and the life of God will pour out of you, transforming your life.

Let Christ live through you, and you will discover the real meaning, purpose, and joy of life as God intends it to be.

Chapter 6

Renewing the Mind

Be renewed in the spirit of your mind.
Ephesians 4:23

As a result of some teaching that has taken place in the past few years, many Christians have started putting new information into their minds. They now know intellectually that it is by the stripes of Jesus they were healed (1 Pet. 2:24). But they still see themselves sick; they still think they are infirm. They have changed their knowledge, but they haven't let that knowledge change their outlook. Their viewpoint hasn't changed. They have new information in their minds, but they don't have a new way of thinking. It is vitally important to see the difference.

In Ephesians 4:24, Paul tells us to be renewed in the spirit of our minds. The New International Version says we are to be made new in the attitude of our minds. The Amplified Bible says we are to have a fresh mental and spiritual attitude. So, in this verse, Paul is not just talking about *what* we think but also the *way* we think—our attitudes and our entire outlook on life.

For instance, pessimism is an attitude just as optimism is an attitude. Given the same facts, a pessimist and an optimist will have totally different mental dispositions. They have programmed themselves to respond differently to those facts. A pessimist will look at a situation and focus on the negative side of it, while an optimist will look at the same situation and focus on the positive side.

In order to manage our emotions, we must change the way we think. We have got to recognize that with Jesus Christ on our side, we now have a supernatural ability we didn't have before we came to know Him as Savior and Lord. We need to quit comparing ourselves with the world and expecting the same results the people of the world expect, because the people of the world do not have God actively involved in their lives.

God wants to be involved in everyone's life. To most people, He is on the outside, whereas with us as believers, He now lives on the inside. God has deposited His life and His supernatural ability on the inside of us; therefore, there needs to be an entire attitude change within us. As our attitude changes, our emotions follow along and change with it. Our emotions follow 100 percent what we think and how we think.

We have already established these truths in Proverbs 23:7, Romans 8:6, and Isaiah 26:3. Review these scriptures to see how they relate to your emotions.

Thinking in Pictures

For as he thinketh in his heart, so is he.
Proverbs 23:7

This shows us in greater detail how our thoughts affect every part of our everyday lives. I once heard someone say that every person has a picture on the inside of themselves. They picture not only themselves but everything around them.

We think in pictures. If I asked you to think of an apple, you would see an apple in your head. You wouldn't picture the word *apple*; you would picture the real thing—the object itself. That image could be refined with words. If I asked you to think of a big red apple, that is what you would see rather than a small green apple. I could even change it further by asking you to think of a dry, overripe apple. Immediately you would start imagining the apple being all shriveled up. I could say there is a worm coming out of the apple, and that would paint yet another picture in your mind.

Words spoken from the outside paint pictures on the inside, and pictures on the inside determine actions on the outside.

Each one of us has a picture of ourselves. It's like a snapshot on the inside of us of who we are. That inward picture determines the way we act and react to things on the outside.

For instance, if you see yourself as an angry, violent person, then you are going to behave and react accordingly. If you see yourself as a brute, you are going to act like a brute. If you see yourself as insecure, inadequate, weak, and incompetent, you will have no confidence in yourself at all. The mental image you have of yourself will dictate your response when a challenge comes your way.

People can be placed in the same situation, yet respond to it differently. For instance, if different people are confronted separately by a mugger, some will respond violently. They will become so strong and resist so hard that they will intimidate the mugger and drive them off. Others in that same situation will respond in fear and timidity, totally withdrawing from any possible conflict. Some may even have an extreme reaction by fainting, panicking, or becoming hysterical.

The exact same situation can cause radically different reactions because of the differences in the way each person thinks and the way they view themselves. You could probably determine what mental image they have of themselves simply by their reactions.

Your life is departmentalized, and every area has a self-image. That image dictates the way you respond emotionally and physically to every situation in life. Again, your emotions are determined by your thoughts and perceptions.

You may try to hide your true feelings, and you may hide them very well for a time. But eventually, your true thoughts and emotions will surface, and your actions will reflect those thoughts. No one can consistently perform differently from the way they think—the picture they have of themselves.

How Do You See Yourself?

And there we saw the giants, the sons of Anak, which come of the giants: and we were in our own sight as grasshoppers, and so we were in their sight.

Numbers 13:33

When the children of Israel faced a powerful enemy, they saw themselves as grasshoppers. They became so fearful, they refused to go in and take the land God had promised them. As a result, God led them back into the wilderness until that entire faithless generation had died off.

When a powerful enemy is standing before you in the form of trials and tribulations, how do you see yourself? Do you shrink from the God-given power and authority that is in you, or do you boldly stand up to that enemy and proclaim the promises of God?

It doesn't matter how your enemy sees you. The important thing is how you see yourself. The Israelites saw themselves as grasshoppers. That's what defeated them. In contrast, David saw the giant Goliath not as a giant but as someone without God's covenant (1 Sam. 17:36). He saw Goliath as only having physical strength, while he himself had God's strength.

When I was drafted into the army, I was put in a situation where there was ungodliness around me that I had never been exposed to before. There was great pressure on me to conform.

At times, I was literally the only person who had any moral foundation at all.

For example, while I was in Vietnam, the United States government actually paid for Filipino women to be brought into what was called a "standdown area" by the troops sent there for R & R. Technically, these women were performers: they would sing, dance, and entertain the troops. But in reality, they were prostitutes. The government supplied all the liquor the troops could drink and provided little shacks where they could party, drink, and have sex with these prostitutes. There were times when I was literally the only person out of hundreds who didn't participate in that activity. As I sat there by myself, many times I would be mocked, ridiculed, and made fun of. Believe me; I felt the pressure!

Many of those men were considered to be upstanding, moral citizens in the United States. But when they got over there and were separated from everything and everyone they knew, they became so lonely and pressured that they did things they would never have done at home. Why? Because they didn't have a firm, established direction for their lives. Many of them would never have lived a life like that in the United States, but when they got into that negative situation, they found themselves sucked into that lifestyle. They did things that I am sure they now regret and are ashamed of, things they have probably never shared with anyone else. Their problem was that because they had such a weak self-image, they allowed themselves to be shaped into the wrong mold.

> **Be not conformed to this world: but be ye transformed by the renewing of your mind, that ye may prove what is that good, and acceptable, and perfect, will of God.**
>
> *Romans 12:2*

I didn't go the directions of all the others. I was in the exact same situation as the rest of those men, yet I had a different, predisposed attitude. I had already chosen the course for my life, and it kept me from going in the wrong direction. Instead of responding to that situation negatively and being sucked into it, my mindset hardened me and made me that much more committed to the path God had already shown me to be right for my life.

I once heard an army chaplain put it this way: "Sure, the army's a fire, and it'll melt you, but you'll fit into whatever mold you've already picked for yourself."

That is exactly what happened to me. By the time I was drafted and sent to Vietnam, I had already made a total commitment of my life to the Lord. I was determined to live for Him with everything I had. Every pressure that came my way just drove me that much closer to God. Other people there had been mediocre Christians before they went to war. They weren't bad people, and they hadn't done anything particularly wrong, but they had not set their minds and committed themselves totally to the way they knew to be right. As a result, as soon as the pressure came, they melted into the mold of everyone around them.

As Christians, that is not the mold we are to be conformed to. We are to be conformed to the image of Christ by renewing our minds to the Word of God.

Your Mindset Determines the Outcome

Emotionally conforming to something other than God's Word happens to Christians all the time. They end up conforming their lives to a standard they never would have chosen for themselves on their own, because they don't have their lives already planned in their minds. They don't see themselves as total overcomers in any certain area. They may have knowledge about it, but they still view themselves as failures. They still view themselves as losers in some area, and it turns out to be a self-fulfilling prophecy.

This is evident in the area of finances. I know a certain woman whose husband died and left her enough money that she should have been satisfied for the rest of her life. This woman was already in her sixties, but within a year, she was in poverty. She had spent some of the money wisely, but the majority of it was just blown away.

You may ask, "How could that happen?" It happened because this woman grew up in poverty. For a large portion of their lives, she and her husband had been alcoholics before they were born again. They had lived that way so long, it had become a mindset on the inside of them. Although they had amassed some money over their lifetime, they still saw themselves as poor. They talked poor. They acted poor. They bought the cheapest things available. They had an attitude of poverty. Although the wife inherited all of her husband's money, within a very short period of time, she was right back where she started because that's the way she saw herself.

Proverbs 23:7 says that whatever we think in our hearts, that is what we are. It doesn't say that as we think in our hearts, it has an influence on our lives and the way things turn out for us. No, it says that's the way we are.

If you are poor, you may think it's because of your skin color. You may think it's because of the social class into which you were born or the geographical area in which you grew up. You may think it's because the government hasn't provided you the right opportunities to prosper. You may think that if you could get more welfare, you wouldn't be in your situation. You may think you're held down because you're not as pretty, as gifted, or as favored as someone else. All of these are excuses. We all have a thousand and one excuses for being as we are. The truth is, if you're poor today, it's because you're *thinking* poor. You see yourself as poor. You act poor. Now, I am not saying that you don't desire to have wealth, but you honestly see yourself poor. If you were put into a situation where you were given great riches, unless you changed your thinking, it would be just a matter of time until you became exactly the way you are now.

On the other hand, if you would take the Word of God and begin to see yourself as God sees you, sooner or later you would become just what you envision. What you think is what you get. It all begins in the mind.

Thinking Precedes Manifestation

For ye know the grace of our Lord Jesus Christ, that, though he was rich, yet for your sakes he became poor, that ye through his poverty might be rich.

2 Corinthians 8:9

If people would read that verse and really begin seeing themselves as prosperous, thinking of themselves as rich in Christ, it would be just a matter of time until that prosperity began to manifest itself in their lives.

When my wife and I first got started in the ministry, we were so poor, we couldn't pay attention! It wasn't because we didn't have money. I was raised in a middle-class home, and when I got married I had thousands of dollars in the bank. I had a good start in life, but I was more zealous than I was wise.

I misunderstood how the scriptural principle of finances worked. I knew I was called to the ministry and couldn't wait to start living by faith. So I took all of those thousands of dollars I had and, within one month's time, *gave* away all that money. Why did I do such a foolish thing? I did it because I wanted to get right to the place where God was meeting all of our of needs supernaturally.

As a friend of mine says, "That is dumb to the second power; it's dumb, dumb." But, nonetheless, that's what I did. As a result of my stupidity, my wife and I experienced some critical poverty in our life together. But I was not raised in poverty. I didn't really see myself poor even though we were having major financial problems.

Our first son, Joshua, was born on March 21. Just before that, in the month of January, our total income was $23.53. In February, it jumped up to $53. Our expense for rent alone was $100 a month, so we were in a critical situation. We were in such dire financial straits that we were going without food.

Yet, during that period of time, it never once occurred to me to go and get food stamps or apply for welfare. I don't know all of the requirements, so I'm not sure whether we would have qualified or not, but we were definitely below the poverty level. There was probably some assistance we could have received, but it never occurred to me to apply for it, because I really believed we were prosperous. I couldn't understand the situation we were in. It took me a while to get it through my thick head that I had caused a lot of my own problems, but God loved me and finally worked me through them.

The point I am making is that even though I was in as critical a financial condition as anyone reading this book right now, I never saw myself poor. I never thought poor. I didn't dress poor. I didn't talk poor. I didn't act poor. And as a result, I eventually came out of that situation.

All during that period, I saw myself prosperous. I knew it was just a matter of time until the Word of God would start working in my life. Now God supplies all my needs according to His riches in glory by Christ Jesus (Phil. 4:19).

See Yourself the Way You Want to Be

You may be thinking, *Man, I could live that way, too, if I could just win the lottery and get a million dollars. Then all my problems would be over!* No, unless you changed your self-image, you would blow that million dollars in no time and be right back where you started. If you won five million dollars, you might last five times as long as the person who won a million dollars, but sooner or later you would lose it all because of your poverty mentality.

I know many people who will say, "But wait a minute. You don't understand—I don't have an education." There are lots of people who don't have an education and are multimillionaires today. A lack of education is not the problem. Now, I'm not saying that education is not a factor, depending on what vocation you're in. Sometimes you have to have an education to progress. I'm not against education at all, but the biggest controlling factor in your prosperity is the way you view yourself—the mental image you have of yourself. If your mental image does not conform to the Word of God, you're not going to get anywhere in life, no matter how educated you are.

Remember, Proverbs 23:7 says that as you think in your heart, that is how you will be. There is no exception to that rule. If you want to be prosperous, you have got to think of yourself as prosperous. If you want to be healthy, you must see yourself healthy. If you want to be strong, form a picture of yourself as strong in God, and don't let go of it!

Thinking Determines Emotions

Your mental image determines your actions because it specifically determines your emotions. When your entire thought process is pure and righteous, you can easily choose good over evil because you are in total control of your emotions. I'm not saying you won't be challenged by trying situations, but you won't be controlled by those situations.

I have learned that I can be a loving person in spite of what others may say about me. The Lord has ministered so much love to me and has led me to share it with others so often that it irritates some people. Some have spoken out against me and even threatened to kill me. They have lied about me and accused me of all kinds of terrible things.

A well-known national minister once branded me as a Jim Jones. He said my ministry was the biggest cult that ever existed. And yet, I can honestly say that I never had one bitter attitude toward that person or any of the others who opposed me and attacked me. I have walked in love. I have even held meetings with that minister and have told that person that I love him and that there is no problem between us. Those accusations have had no negative impact on my life whatsoever.

Now, that kind of loving attitude didn't come overnight; it came because I made a commitment to love rather than to hate. I have preprogrammed myself that if someone hates me, I am not going to hate back. I may not like it. I may not get blessed by it. But I am not going to get out of the Spirit over it. I choose to walk in love.

No one is going to change the way I feel, because my joy and my peace are tied 100 percent to the Lord Jesus Christ and what He has done in my life. I refuse to give that up for anyone or anything.

There are times when it takes more effort than usual to walk in love. If a person I really admire and respect comes out against me and hurts me, walking in love toward that individual may take some extra effort. I may have to literally shut myself off from everyone to fast and pray and focus my attention on the Lord. It may take a lot of time and effort, but I can guarantee you that's what I'm going to do. I am not going to be depressed because of the negatives things I have to contend with in my life and ministry.

If I allowed myself, I could be in a constant state of turmoil because, like everyone else, I have a lot of problems. Ministers are not immune to problems. In fact, I believe that when you're a minister, more people hate you than if you were in any other profession. But how you handle that situation depends upon where your focus is.

The way you think controls everything. The image you have on the inside is a product of your thinking. It determines your emotions, and your emotions determine your actions. That's why it's so important to have a positive, Christ-centered self-image despite what's going on around you. And the way to develop that positive self-image is by being renewed in the spirit of your mind—staying focused on God and applying His Word to every area of your life.

Chapter 7

Who Are You?

I have established a basic outline of the truth that there is the new you and the old you. The new you has the mind of Christ and all the abilities of Christ. You have the picture of yourself in Christ; now you need to finish coloring it in. It's not enough to know that there is a new you. You have to have more details before you can actually see what has happened to you in your spirit man.

To get an accurate mental image of your physical features, you look in a mirror or make a photograph or video of yourself. Did you know that when you do that, you are using faith? It takes faith to look at a mirror, a photo, or a video and say, "That's me." How do you know for sure the image you are seeing is really you?

Many people think that's a ridiculous question. Yet I remember a professor I had in my first year of college who asked that very question. He was trying to get us to drop all of our preconceived ideas and come into the class with open minds. So he took a chair, set it in front of us, and systematically tried to prove to us that the chair wasn't there.

Of course, on the surface everyone said, "Well, that's stupid; I can see it." But then he started reasoning. "How do you know that what you're seeing is true?" he asked. "How do you know your eyes are accurately interpreting to your brain the things you're seeing? How do you know you don't have some kind of a problem that causes you to see things that aren't really there?"

He was challenging things that most people never really think about. By the time we left his class, if we had followed his line of reasoning, we couldn't have proved that the chair was there after all.

That kind of reasoning is prevalent in our society today. We have challenged basic foundational principles that we should accept by faith. God's Word is truth, and we ought to accept it as such (John 17:17).

When it comes to looking in a mirror, most of us have never challenged the validity of what we see. We are seeing a reflection that we see by faith, believing it to be us. But it only *represents* us. It's not the *real* us. For instance, we don't know for sure that we have hair on the top of our heads.

Now, you may say, "Oh, yes, I do. I've seen it in the mirror."

No, what you've seen is a reflection of the hair on your head.

"Well, I can feel it with my physical hands."

Maybe so, but you still haven't seen it. How do you know that what you feel is accurate?

One way or the other, you are taking something by faith. The same thing happens when we look at our spirits. We can't see our spirits in a mirror, so how can we accurately view our spirits?

There are some people who depend upon their senses so much, they can't accept that there is any realm of reality except what they can see, taste, hear, smell, or feel. Because they can't physically sense their spirits, they give up trying. "It's hopeless," they say. "I don't really understand spiritual things." It's because they are looking in the wrong place.

<u>God's Mirror</u>

The words that I speak unto you, they are spirit, and they are life.

John 6:63

If the words Jesus spoke were spirit and life, then the Word of God is not just a book; it's a look into the spiritual realm. It's like a spiritual mirror we use to see spiritual truth.

If we want to see if our hair is combed, we look in a mirror, trusting that the representation we see is true. In the same way, if we want to see what our spirits are like, we go to God's Word and see what God says about us, trusting that whatever He says about us is the way we are—whether we feel it or not.

We may not feel like our hair is combed, but that really has nothing to do with whether it is combed or not. Someone may be able to convince us with their words that our hair is messed up, when in truth it really is combed. So we can't go by our feelings; we have to look and see for ourselves and trust that what we see is true.

It's the same thing with the sprit man. You may have read in the Bible, **"I can do all things through Christ which strengtheneth me"** (Phil. 4:13.) You may know that intellectually, but you don't feel it. So when you come up against a problem, you feel like, "Oh, man, I don't have any power." But it doesn't matter what you *feel*, if you are going by what God's Word says. The truth is that whatever God's Word *says* about you is spirit and it is life—it is spiritual truth.

Be ye doers of the word, and not hearers only, deceiving your own selves.
For if any be a hearer of the word, and not a doer, he is like unto a man beholding his natural face in a glass:

For he beholdeth himself, and goeth his way, and straightway forgetteth what manner of man he was.

But whoso looketh into the perfect law of liberty, and continueth therein, he being not a forgetful hearer, but a doer of the work, this man shall be blessed in his deed.

James 1:22-25

James talks about a man who looks in a mirror and sees his natural face, then goes his way and immediately forgets what he looks like. But James also says that anyone who looks into the perfect law of liberty (God's Word) and continues in it will be blessed.

Just as we look in a mirror to see our physical selves, we look into God's Word to see our spiritual self.

When a person makes Jesus Christ the Lord of their life, there is a transformation that takes place on the inside. Most Christians know this in their minds, but very few of them have ever gotten an accurate mental picture, or perception, of who they really are in the spirit. Because they don't have the correct information about who they are in Christ, they can only operate on the information they *do* have, and they naturally act out of their old selves. They act out of their old abilities instead of their newfound abilities in Christ. This is where so many Christians miss God's best for them.

Most Christians have the desire to do the right things, but they feel unequipped. They feel they don't have the ability. I know of many Christians who are praying for faith, power, and all kinds of spiritual gifts. The truth is, according to God's Word they already have them—all believers have them.

Now, you may say, "But wait a minute. I don't have these things. I know this because I don't feel them." It doesn't have anything to do with what you *feel*; it has to do with what you *believe*.

The Law of Faith

Christians who cry out to the Lord "O God, please give me faith" are going to be totally shocked when they get to heaven and discover they had the exact same faith Jesus had while He was here on this earth.

We don't need more faith. What we need is the realization of what we already have in Christ Jesus. That's the first step. Then once we know we have faith, we need to learn the spiritual laws that govern it.

> **Where is boasting then? It is excluded. By what law? of works? Nay: but by the law of faith.**
> ***Romans 3:27***

In this scripture, Paul talks about the law of faith. If you are truly born again, you have the same faith in you that Jesus had, but there are laws that govern it. There are certain things you need to do to release that faith. It's just like the law of electricity. Electricity exists, but you have to know how to cooperate with it and use it. After you know you have it, there are things you need to learn to draw on it and operate in it.

Most Christians are perishing for a lack of knowledge (Hos. 4:6). They don't know who they are in Christ, so they are guided and directed by their feelings or emotions. Spiritual truth cannot be perceived by feelings. It can't be seen in a physical mirror. The Word of God is the only way to tap into it, and most Christians are woefully ignorant of what God's Word has to say about them. Because they don't know who they are in Christ Jesus, they are missing out on everything God's Word has for them.

We have established the fact that there are two of us—the old man and the new man. But which one is the real us? What is our identity? Most people would say, "It's the part of us that feels fearful, weak, and inadequate—that's the real us." No, the real us is that born-again us, the part of us that is going to live for all eternity. That old self that feels fearful, weak, and inadequate is going to eventually die and be replaced. Right now the real us, the only part of us that is born again, is the spirit within.

If you don't know who you are in Christ, you are trying to live out of your old man, and you're going to be frustrated and sadly disappointed. There is a new you, and you've got to find out who you are and the power that is there for you.

When I was in Vietnam, I went through an experience that I will never forget. It happened not long after I got there, when everything was still fairly new to me. I was with about ten other American soldiers on top of a hill surrounded by about five thousand well-armed, well-equipped, and well-trained North Vietnamese Army troops. We were put on red alert. At night we could see the muzzle fire from the NVA rifles, and it looked like they were going to overrun our hill.

Everyone was supposed to stay awake all night. I was in a bunker with four other guys, and they all went to sleep while I stayed awake on watch. When it came their time to pull guard duty, I couldn't get them up. "Leave me alone," they all told me, so I wound up staying awake all night pulling guard duty because I felt like we could be overrun at any time.

Then the second night came around, and by this time I was worn to a frazzle. But those guys still weren't pulling their guard duty. Finally, I asked them, "What's wrong? Don't you guys realize this is a critical situation? There are 5,000 of the enemy and only 120 of us. We could be killed at any moment." They just started laughing.

"You must be new in this country," they said.

"Yes, I am," I answered.

So they started telling me about the superior firepower we had on that hill. Even though there were only 120 of us, we had many times more firepower than the enemy. As they described it in detail, it was so convincing, I realized, "I'm not excited about this war, but if we've got to fight it, I'd just as soon have the enemy come out of their holes and fight us on our terms." I developed the attitude, *Come on—I dare you*. I lost all my fear, all my worry, and all my concern. That night I actually got so sleepy, I couldn't stay awake. Since I could no longer pull everyone else's guard duty, I just fell asleep.

The point is that when you understand who you are in Christ and the authority and power you have in Him, your attitude will change. Instead of being intimidated by your problems, you will be confident. Instead of being full of worry, fear, doubt, and care, you will experience totally different emotions. That knowledge will change the way you think, and therefore it will change the way you feel.

This is how the law of faith works: You look into the law of liberty, God's Word, which is your mirror. You see yourself through God's eyes, as He sees you in Christ, and you choose to believe and adopt His picture of you. Then you meditate on that picture day and night—don't let go of it.

When you operate in the law of faith, you see yourself as God sees you—powerful in Him, prosperous in Him, healthy in Him, and wise in Him. Then the law of faith produces what you believe in your everyday life.

<u>You Are a New Spirit</u>

Therefore if any man be in Christ, he is a new creature: old things are passed away; behold, all things are become new.

2 Corinthians 5:17

Identifying who you really are in Christ and living in accordance with that identity is the key to the Christian life. The key to understanding who you are in Christ is recognizing that it is your spirit that is born again. It is your spirit that has changed.

> **I pray God your whole spirit and soul and body be preserved blameless unto the coming of our Lord Jesus Christ.**
> *1 Thessalonians 5:23*

According to this scripture, we have three parts—a spirit, a soul, and a body. Paul prayed that God would keep and preserve the Thessalonians wholly, or completely, in *spirit, soul,* and *body.*

The body is very easy to identify. It is the physical part of us. The soul is the emotional part, or what most people consider to be their real personality. It includes our thinking processes, our feelings, and our wills. Then there's another part of us that the Bible calls the spirit, and this is actually the most important part.

In James 2:26, the Bible tells us that **"as the body without the spirit is dead, so faith without works is dead also."** The spirit is the dynamo of our whole beings. It is the life-giving force within us.

> **And the LORD God formed man of the dust of the ground, and breathed into his nostrils the breath of life; and man became a living soul.**
> *Genesis 2:7*

When the Bible says God created Adam and breathed into him the breath of life, that word **"breath"** is the same word from which we get the word *spirit.* God put a spirit on the inside of Adam, and that's when life came. When the spirit leaves, that's when life leaves. So the spirit is the real part of us, and when we become born again, we receive new spirits.

And the Lord God commanded the man, saying, Of every tree in the garden thou mayest freely eat:

But of the tree of the knowledge of good and evil, thou shalt not eat of it: for in the day that thou eatest thereof thou shalt surely die.

Genesis 2:16-17

The Lord told Adam that in the day he ate of the fruit of the Tree of the Knowledge of Good and Evil, he would surely die. When Adam disobeyed God and ate of that forbidden fruit, his spirit died within him. He didn't die physically for 930 years, but he died spiritually at that exact moment. That doesn't mean his spirit ceased to exist. It was still there. But it ceased to be under the control of the Lord. It was no longer releasing the life of God, which made it incapable of sustaining physical life forever.

The spirit of man received the life of God and then disseminated it through the soul and body. When Adam sinned against God and did his own thing, the spirit within him was separated from fellowship with God. He no longer had the divine life of God—the Holy Spirit—flowing through him. Sadly, another spirit stepped in to take its place, which was Satan, who began to pour his death into the human race through the spirit.

The spirit was within man from Adam until salvation was united with the devil. That's what Paul was referring to when he wrote in Ephesians 2:2-3 that before we were saved, we were by nature the children of disobedience, the children of wrath; i.e., the children of the devil. He meant that until we were born again, our spirits were united with the devil, and Satan poured his corruption into us through our spirit man.

As we saw in 2 Corinthians 5:17, when we become born again, we become new creatures, or new creations. Old things pass away, and all things become new. Just by the process of elimination, we understand that it is not talking about our physical bodies, because when we were born again our physical bodies did not change. If we were fat before we got saved, we were still fat after we got saved. That's not the part of us that changes through salvation.

Neither do our souls change, because as we saw in 1 Corinthians 13:9-10 that now we only know in part, we only prophesy in part, but when that which is perfect is come, then we will know all things just as we are known. The mental part of us is not saved. If we were ignorant before we got saved, we'll be ignorant after we got saved, until we educate ourselves through the Word of God.

If our physical bodies didn't change and our souls didn't change, then the only part of us that's left is the spirit. Our spirits were completely and radically changed when we were born again. We didn't just get improved; we became totally brand-new spirits. The Christian life derives its power from this new birth. When we were born again, God placed a new spirit on the inside of us, and we have everything we need to live the victorious Christian life.

Our born-again spirits have everything, and they will never change. We are the exact same spirits at this moment that we will be in eternity. When we go to be with the Lord, our spirits aren't going to be improved upon, and we're not going to have to be changed again. We are as complete right this moment as we will ever be in all eternity.

That is an awesome thing to think about! We have eternity living inside of us!

Acknowledge Your Identity

If we could really get a vision that our spirit man is complete, it would change many of our emotions and our actions. Most of us see ourselves in light of eternity as being different. We think that when we get to heaven, we'll see that everything we experience on earth was worth it. We sing songs like "Farther along we'll know all about it." Many Christians really believe that in heaven, there is going to be a total transformation, and we are going to become something special. But they don't see themselves as being complete in Christ right now.

A transformation will take place in the physical realm and in the soulish realm when we go to heaven, but in the spiritual realm, we are right this moment the way we will be throughout all eternity. Our spirits are as complete right now as they will ever be. One-third of our salvation is through—it's over, it's complete. We don't have to wait to get to heaven to see that God created our spirit man special and complete.

If you can get a vision of that truth and renew your mind accordingly, perceiving yourself and acting the way you really are in your born-again self, then you will experience the life that is already in your spirit. You can experience all that right here in the physical realm to the degree that you renew your mind through God's Word and let your spirit man reign and rule over your natural man. It will make a huge difference in your life and your emotions.

> **I thank my God, making mention of thee always in my prayers,**
> **Hearing of thy love and faith, which thou hast toward the Lord Jesus, and toward all saints;**
> **That the communication of thy faith may become effectual by the acknowledging of every good thing which is in you in Christ Jesus.**
> *Philemon 4-6*

In this passage Paul basically says the same thing I have been saying in this book. In order to made your faith effectual, you have to acknowledge the good things that are in you in Christ Jesus.

Notice the terminology—Paul says, "Acknowledge." You can't acknowledge something that doesn't already exist. Most Christians have the mistaken idea that what they need is out there somewhere in heaven. They think that it is their job to try to get what they need from God and bring it to themselves. But that's not what the Bible teaches.

We're not to go looking for something we hope exists. The Bible doesn't say that our faith becomes effectual by getting God to put His life into us. No, it's already there. It's just a matter of *acknowledging* it.

Once you are born again, the rest of the Christian life is simply renewing your mind and acting according to who you are in Christ, which releases the life of God on the inside of you.

Paul uses the same terminology in Colossians 2:2 where he prays for those in Colosse and Laodicea **"that their hearts might be comforted, being knit together in love, and unto all riches of the full assurance of understanding, to the acknowledgment of the mystery of God, and of the Father, and of Christ."**

Paul speaks of **"the full assurance of understanding."** Now, you can't be assured of something that isn't already a reality, and you can't understand something that doesn't exist. Paul also uses the expression **"the acknowledgement of the mystery."** Both of these terms refer to getting a revelation of something that already exists. We have already seen in Colossians 1:27 that this mystery is Christ in you, the hope of glory. It is not "Christ is going to be in you," but rather "Right now, Christ is in you, the hope of glory."

In Ephesians 1:18, Paul prayed for the believers in Ephesus that the eyes of their understanding might be enlightened so they could know the hope of their calling and the riches of the glory of their inheritance *in the saints*.

God's inheritance isn't in heaven somewhere; it's in us. God Himself lives on the inside of us. We don't have just a little dab of heaven. We don't have just a tiny bit of salvation, just enough to let us squeak by. In our spirits, our salvation is complete. Our spirits are as holy, as righteous, and as pure as they will ever get. Our inheritance is inside of us. We don't need to close our eyes and picture heaven with its streets of gold or great piles of money and wealth. We already have all that.

> **For in him** [Christ] **dwelleth all the fullness of the Godhead bodily.**
> **And ye are complete in him, which is the head of all principality and power.**
> *Colossians 2:9-10, brackets mine*

The power and the glory that indwells you would bankrupt heaven. You have everything that is in heaven because you have Jesus, and in Jesus are hid all the treasures of wisdom and knowledge (Col. 2:3). Jesus is the fullness of the Godhead bodily, and you are complete in Him. Praise God, your spirit is so perfect, righteous, holy, and pure that you can't get any better.

Open Your Eyes to the Power Within You!

> [I] **cease not to give thanks for you, making mention of you in my prayers,**
> **That the God of our Lord Jesus Christ, the Father of glory, may give unto you the spirit of wisdom and revelation in the knowledge of him:**
> **The eyes of your understanding being enlightened; that ye may know what is the hope of his calling, and what the riches of the glory of his inheritance in the saints,**
> **And what is the exceeding greatness of his power to us-ward who believe, according to** [in the proportion, or to the degree] **the working of his mighty power, Which he wrought in Christ, when he raised him from the dead, and set him at his own right hand in the heavenly places.**
> *Ephesians 1:16-20, brackets mine*

Paul is saying, "Open your eyes to the fact that you have the same power on the inside of you that raised Jesus Christ from the dead."

If you could measure the different displays of God's power, I guarantee you, raising Jesus from the dead was the greatest manifestation of God's power that ever took place—and you have that same power on the inside of you right now! It's not off in the future; it's already there. Your spirit is 100 percent complete.

> **That which is born of the flesh is flesh; and that which is born of the Spirit is spirit.**
> *John 3:6*

You may say, "How can this be? If I have God Himself living on the inside of me and if I have the same awesome power in me that raised Christ from the dead, then why can't I feel it?" Again, you cannot *feel* the spirit realm. As Jesus told Nicodemus in this scripture, physical things are physical and spiritual things are spiritual. They are two different realms.

You are spirit, but like most Christians, you only perceive the physical, emotional part of you. There is a spirit you on the inside that you cannot feel; you have to believe it. Once you believe it and bring what is a spiritual reality into your physical, mental realm, then you can begin thinking spiritually, and your emotions will correspond and follow the way you think. But if you don't think it, if you can't see it, and if you don't renew your mind, you can have this life of God living in your spirit and never feel it.

If you will renew your mind, your emotions will follow your thinking. They do not follow your spirit. You perceive what God's Word says by faith, taking it as being spiritual truth and believing it. Then your emotions follow what you think. If you think you're just a nothing, you're a no one, and you don't have any power, then your emotions will reflect that. But if you begin to see who you are in Christ and renew your mind to that truth, your emotions will correspond and go along with it.

> **And that ye put on the new man, which after
> God is created in righteousness and true holiness.**
> *Ephesians 4:24*

> **For he [God] hath made him [Jesus] to be sin
> for us, who knew no sin; that we might be made
> the righteousness of God in him.**
> *2 Corinthians 5:21, brackets mine*

How holy do you think your spirit is? Your spirit, which is your new man, was created in righteousness and true holiness. You didn't just get a little bit of righteousness when you got saved; you *are* the righteousness of God.

Again, I'm not talking about the physical man. Some Christians just choke when anyone starts talking about this subject of them being the righteousness of God. When I say that we have been made the righteousness of God, they look at the soulish realm—the physical, mental, and emotional part—and say, "I am not righteous! I still have rotten thoughts. I still get angry and depressed. I'm like this and you say I'm righteous?" Then they begin to condemn me, saying, "That's not true. I won't be righteous until I go to be with the Lord."

But these scriptures are talking about the spirit. The spirit is the part of you that is righteous and truly holy. Your spirit man has been created in righteousness and holiness.

> **Herein is our love made perfect, that we may
> have boldness in the day of judgment: because as
> he is, so are we in this world.**
> *1 John 4:17*

That is such an awesome scripture that most people read it and say, "Man, the Bible is so hard to understand, because I can guarantee you, I'm not as Jesus is. I don't look like Him, I don't talk like Him, and I don't act like Him!"

If you look at your physical self in the mirror, you are likely to say, "Is this what Jesus looks lie? You see wrinkles or zits or something you aren't pleased with, and you think, *This just can't be what Jesus looks like! I just can't understand the Bible.*

The reason you have problems understanding the Bible is because the Bible is a spiritual book and speaks in a spiritual language (1 Cor. 2:12-14). When it says "As He is, so are we in this world," it's not talking about your body; it's talking about your spirit. Your born-again spirit is exactly as Jesus is because your spirit has become one with Him.

<u>You Are One with Jesus</u>

He that is joined unto the Lord is one spirit.
1 Corinthians 6:17

In this verse, the Greek word translated **"one"** is *heis*, and it means "one to the exclusion of another" (James Strong's, *The Exhaustive Concordance of the Bible* [Nashville: Abingdon, 1890], "Greek Dictionary of the New Testament," #1520). It doesn't mean one in principle or one in purpose; it means one in actuality. It is the same word used in Ephesians 4:5, which says that there is **"one Lord, one faith, one baptism."** We know there aren't multiple gods. There's only one God. He manifests Himself in three persons, but He is one—one to the exclusion of another. There is no other. This same God says that he who is joined to the Lord is one spirit.

Our spirits have become so united with Jesus that they are identical to the Spirit of the Lord Jesus Christ. The Bible says that **"as he is, so are we in this world"** (1 John 4:17). It doesn't say, "So are we going to be." That's the way religion has interpreted that scripture—that some day we are going to be like Him. But the truth is, in our spirits, we are exactly as He is right now.

> **However, you are not in the flesh but in the
> Spirit, if indeed the Spirit of God dwells in you.
> But if anyone does not have the Spirit of Christ,
> he does not belong to Him.**
>
> *Romans 8:9, NASB*

> **Because ye are sons, God hath sent forth
> the Spirit of his Son into your hearts, crying,
> Abba, Father.**
>
> *Galatians 4:6*

Our born-again spirits are literally *the* Spirit of Christ. When
we are born again, the new spirit we receive is actually the Spirit of
Christ. It is our spirits, and it is His Spirit. They are joined together
as one. Everything that can be said about the Spirit of Jesus is also
true of our born-again spirits.

I know some people who freak out at this concept. They get
upset and say, "Man, you can't believe that. You're saying that
you're a god." No, not in my physical person. In my soulish person,
definitely not. But in my born-again spirit, I have become united
with the Lord, and I am as complete in my spirit at this exact
moment as I will be in eternity. My spirit isn't going to be changed
or improved. It is perfected right this moment, and so is yours.

You Are Sanctified—Forever

> **By the which will** [God's will] **we are sanctified
> through the offering of the body of Jesus Christ
> once for all.**
> **And every priest standeth daily ministering
> and offering oftentimes the same sacrifices, which
> can never take away sins:**
> **But this man, after he had offered one sacrifice
> for sins for ever, sat down on the right hand
> of God;**

> **From henceforth expecting till his enemies be made his footstool.**
> **For by one offering he hath perfected for ever them that are sanctified.**
> *Hebrews 10:10-14, brackets mine*

When Jesus died on the cross, He put into effect a will and a testament that sanctified us once and for all. That doesn't mean that one offering worked for everyone; it means that one offering works for each individual who receives it—forever. There's no need for an offering or a sacrifice to be made over and over again.

Jesus' sacrifice dealt with sin **"once for all"** (Heb. 10:10). His sacrifice was made **"for sins for ever"** (Heb. 10:12). By the sacrifice of Himself on the cross **"he hath perfected for ever them that are sanctified"** (Heb. 10:14). This scripture tells us that if we have accepted Jesus, we have been sanctified once and for all, perfected forever. There is no need for additional sacrifices. Jesus paid a one-time price for our righteousness.

Yet some people will say, "Man, that doesn't make sense, because I still have so many problems in my life." That may be true in the physical, mental, and emotional realms, but in the spiritual realm, you are sanctified and perfected forever. Your spirit is forgiven of sin forever. You're perfect, holy, and righteous in your spirit. There is nothing impure in your spirit.

This scripture tells us that our spirits hve been made perfect. Viewing this in light of Hebrews 10:10-14, we can see that our spirit man was made perfect—not just temporarily but forever.

So, regardless of how you may feel physically or emotionally, you *are* righteous. You are the very righteousness of God in Christ Jesus, who has sanctified you and made you spiritually perfect, pure, and holy—now and forever. You are one spirit with Him, and as He is in this world, so are you. That is who you are!

Chapter 8

Operating with Your New Mind

But ye have an unction from the Holy One, and ye know all things.

1 John 2:20

As some people read this scripture, their reaction is, "Man, what is the Bible saying? It's so hard to understand. I certainly don't know everything. I can prove that by my test scores." What these people are talking about is their soulish realm.

In the spirit, we Christians have an unction, a special anointing from God, and therefore we know all things. There isn't anything we don't know or cannot call to remembrance, because we have the mind of Christ.

But we have the mind of Christ.

1 Corinthians 2:16

You may read this scripture and say, "If I have the mind of Christ, where is it? It surely doesn't seem to help me in my life."

The mind of Christ is in your spirit. To benefit from it, you have to draw it out. How do you do that? By the Word of God, which is Spirit. The Word of God is the mind of Christ put into physical print. As you read it and the Holy Spirit illuminates it to you, the wisdom that is located in your spirit begins to come out, benefiting your physical mind, your emotions, and your actions.

Drawing on God's Wisdom

Ye have put off the old man with his deeds;
And have put on the new man, which is renewed in knowledge after the image of him that created him.
Colossians 3:9-10

When Paul says we have put off the old man and have put on the new man, this is the same terminology he used before to distinguish between our old, unregenerate spirits and our new, born-again spirits. Our new man—the new spirit within us—is renewed in the knowledge after the image of the one who created it—Jesus Christ.

We have the mind of Christ in our spirits giving us the same wisdom and knowledge of God who created us. We have an unction from the Holy One, and we know all things. We just need to learn to access that wisdom and knowledge.

For the LORD giveth wisdom: out of his mouth cometh knowledge and understanding.
He layeth up sound wisdom for the righteous: he is a buckler to them that walk uprightly.
Proverbs 2:6-7

Therefore with joy shall ye draw water out of the wells of salvation.
Isaiah 12:3

You might say, "Well, that wisdom is found in the spirit. My brain is in the physical. The tests I have to take in school, the work I have to do on my job, the problems I have to solve in my daily life, all of these things are physical. What benefit is it to me to have the mind of Christ in my spirit if I'm living in a physical world?"

Knowing that the mind of Christ is within you is the first step toward reaping those benefits. Once you know it is there, the Bible teaches that you can access that wisdom and knowledge. And there are many ways to do that. Speaking in tongues is one way to draw on the wisdom and knowledge of God. Some people think that speaking in tongues is just something Christians do to prove they have the Holy Spirit. But as you speak in tongues, you are actually drawing on the wisdom and knowledge of God (1 Cor. 14:2).

Once you understand that the mind of Christ is within you, you can begin to make withdrawals from it. But if you don't know it's there, you will never draw on it. If you didn't know you had any money in the bank, you would never write a check. The first step is knowing what your balance is. Then you've got to know how to draw from that account and obtain that money.

Suppose you had a well with water in it. In order to satisfy your thirst, you would have to figure out a way to get the water out of the well. You would need a bucket and some way to let it down and draw it back up. But first of all, you would have to know the well is there, and that there is good water in it. It is possible that someone could die of thirst right next to a well if they didn't have any way of drawing out the water. It is the same with God's wisdom. The first step to accessing His wisdom is knowing it is there for you. He wants to impart divine wisdom to you.

> **Ye shall know the truth, and the truth shall make you free.**
> *John 8:32*

Most Christians don't know what's on the inside of them. Therefore, they don't even know they have an option. When depression comes, most believers don't realize that their spirits are always rejoicing and praising God and that they can draw on and live from that. So they think there's no hope.

"What's the use, Lord?" they pray. "I have been asking You to take away my problems, but it hasn't happened. Here I am, miserable and depressed. I might as well accept my situation and adjust to my circumstance." But that is just not an option to me anymore. I know the truth, and the truth has set me free, just as Jesus said it would (John 8:32).

I remember an instance when I was pastoring a church, and things weren't going my way. People were doing terrible things to me. I tried to resist discouragement and depression, but it just wasn't working. Finally, one evening I felt like giving up and accepting that depression. I was waiting for Jamie and the boys to go to bed so I could have a pity party. I was looking forward to getting down on myself, griping, complaining, and telling God how disappointed I was, but the Lord started bringing to my mind the very things I am sharing with you in this book.

In my flesh, I wanted that depression so I could have a pity party, but all of a sudden, I was presented with the truth from God's Word that I had a choice: Was I going to operate in the flesh or in the spirit? Intellectually, I knew that I should be operating in the spirit, but I felt like being in the flesh. I thought about it for a little while, and ultimately I made the right choice. I said, "Praise God, I don't care what I feel like. I am blessed because God loves me and cares about me." I started building myself up by speaking forth what God's Word says about me. I started thinking about who I am in Christ, and instead of griping, complaining, and having a pity party, I wound up shouting, rejoicing, and having a great time in the Lord. I drew upon God's wisdom.

Every time you are depressed, you have that same option. You may not have known it then, but you know it now. If you didn't know what God's Word says about you, you couldn't draw on it. But now you do know, and from this moment on, if anger, depression, or any negative emotion comes at you, you can take authority over it. You don't have to accept it. You can say, "Wait a minute. This is not according to God's Word. My spirit man is not bummed out. I'm not upset. I'm not angry. I'm not hopeless. My spirit is in charge, and I can choose to let my spirit dominate. I choose to live by my spiritual emotions, not the old carnal emotions. I have the Spirit of God living inside of me, and I choose to walk and live by the spirit, not by the flesh."

What I am sharing with you in this book is really just scratching the surface. There is so much more to share. It takes a lifetime to learn about everything we have in Christ Jesus, to meditate on it, and to let it literally become a part of us.

Drawing upon God's wisdom involves a process. It's not *easy*, but it is *simple*. It's as simple as the fact that you have the life of God in your spirit. In your flesh is where you're experiencing the negative, carnal emotions, and you have a choice. You can either walk in those negative, carnal emotions or you can deny them. You can turn from them and say, "I'm not going to let that happen in me, because I'm a new person in Christ." You can focus your mind on who you are in Christ, what God's Word says about you, and those realities in Christ will manifest themselves in your physical emotions.

That is the truth, and the truth will set you free!

Using Your Faith

The life which I now live in the flesh I live by the faith of the Son of God.
Galatians 2:20

Many Christians know that faith works and that faith has power to change things. They don't doubt any of the testimonies about the great things that have happened in other people's lives, because they believed God. But when it comes to their own situations, they see themselves as faithless because they don't *feel* faith. So they say to the Lord, "O God, please give me faith in this situation." How is God going to give them something He has already given them?

In Galatians 2:20, the Bible teaches us that we have the faith of the Son of God. Galatians 5:22-23 tells us that faith is a fruit of the Spirit that has been given to every believer. In Ephesians 2:8, we saw that it was by grace through faith that we were saved to begin with. If we did not have faith, we would not be born again. That faith has the power to change things. That's why it was given to us.

You already have all of the faith you will ever have or ever need, but it's in your spirit. If you let your feelings tell you otherwise, you will never benefit from that faith. If you perceive yourself as being faithless in your situation, you will say, "I know faith works, but I just don't have any." You will end up defeated again and again. You will continue to go through life intimidated, fearful, filled with worry, care, and anxiety. Your life will continue to be difficult and depressing because that's the way you think.

But if you can begin to renew your mind so that you say "Inside of me, I have the same faith that raised Jesus from the dead, the same faith that Jesus used when He spoke to Lazarus and caused him to come out of the grave," that faith will empower you to do the same things that Jesus did, and even greater things, just as He promised (John 14:12).

> **These things have I written unto you that believe on the name of the Son of God; that ye may know that ye have eternal life, and that ye may believe on the name of the Son of God.**
> *1 John 5:13*

You may have to be honest and just say, "Father, I don't know all of the laws governing faith yet, but I know it's there." Just knowing that it's there will get you excited. It will give you hope that you have what you need though you don't know exactly how to draw it out. Just knowing that it's there will be exciting and encouraging.

There was a time when I desperately needed money. My wife and I were very poor, and when our first son was born, we struggled to keep him fed. We went without food ourselves a lot of times, but we always fed him. We had made a decision that we would never let our son go hungry. It was a time of really putting our faith on the line.

One day it got to where we didn't have enough money to get our son any food for supper. He had eaten earlier that day, but he didn't have anything for the last meal, and I knew we had to come up with something quick.

I was praying and believing God to answer our need. Many times when I prayed, I would expect God to send someone supernaturally. I am a minister, and therefore the people I minister to give back to me financially. It doesn't usually work that way for non-ministers. You may get blessed through your job and through things you set your hand to, but the Bible says **"that they which preach the gospel should live of the gospel"** (1 Cor. 9:14). So I assumed that my money would come through people just coming by.

As I was praying over this need for food for my soon, the Lord spoke to me and said, "You've already got it. It's here. You don't have to have someone come by." All of a sudden, I started thinking, *Well, maybe I left some money in my clothes pockets*. I went through every piece of clothing I had and found nothing. I took the cushions off the sofa and looked behind them. Nothing. Finally, I took the backseat out of the car and found three or four dollars worth of change that had fallen there.

That's not the best example, but it makes my point. I have come a long way since then. I no longer have to search pockets, sofa cushions, or behind car seats to find needed money. But the point is, there was some degree of anxiety as long as I thought that my finances had yet to come. In my own mind, I was sure God was speaking to someone to come by the house and help us out financially, but I wasn't sure they would be obedient, or if they were obedient, whether they would arrive in time for supper. So there was some anxiety even though I was supposedly trusting God to provide what I needed.

Once the Lord spoke to me, "You've already got it—it's just a matter of finding it," all anxiety, fear, and worry left. Instead, there was anticipation, expectation, and hope. I really believed the money was there somewhere, and when I found it, I confirmed my belief.

Ask, Seek, and Knock

And I say unto you, Ask, and it shall be given you; seek, and ye shall find; knock, and it shall be opened unto you.

For every one that asketh receiveth; and he that seeketh findeth; and to him that knocketh it shall be opened.

Luke 11:9-10

And this is the confidence that we have in him, that, if we ask any thing according to his will, he heareth us:

And if we know that he hear us, whatsoever we ask, we know that we have the petitions that we desired of him.

1 John 5:14-15

As long as you approach your situation thinking *O Lord, if I could just have faith or if I could just have peace of mind, I would be all right*; as long as you see spiritual blessings as being on the outside and are constantly asking God for them; there will always be some degree of doubt, anxiety, worry, fear, and care about whether or not you will receive them. But once you understand you already have all of these things, you will quit depending upon your emotions. Once you understand who you are in Christ and begin to see your true identity in Him, all the worry and anxiety will be removed because you will no longer be controlled by your emotions.

That doesn't mean you will never have to go looking, as I did in the backseat of the car. There is going to be a period of time before you actually make the exact connection that releases your answer. But what peace and security it brings just knowing you already have what you are seeking! That's 90 percent of the battle, even if you don't understand everything about how to release it yet.

A good friend of mine used to have a saying: "Even an old blind hog, if he keeps rooting long enough, will come up with something." What he meant by that is that if you know beyond a shadow of a doubt that you have something, and you don't give up, it's just a matter of time until you find it. The key is releasing the faith that God has already given to you, and if you won't quit looking for it, you will eventually hit upon it and see it come to pass. A person who is not totally convinced that they have what they need may try a little bit, but when they don't see results, they will quit because they never really see themselves in possession of it.

In Matthew 13:44, Jesus likened the kingdom of heaven to a treasure hidden in a field, saying that the man sold everything he owned to buy that field because he knew what was buried there. Let's think about that illustration.

Suppose I told you there was a million dollars buried in your backyard. If you had a steam shovel, you could start digging up huge amounts of dirt at one time looking for that money. That would be fairly quick and easy. But if you really believed what I told you, you could eventually get the same results with nothing but a spoon. It would require patience, determination, and a lot of hard work, but if you were so convinced, you wouldn't give up and quit. Then, eventually you would find that million dollars.

But suppose I told the same thing to someone who wasn't fully convinced it was true. If they didn't have the proper equipment, but only a spoon to dig with, they would probably quit after the first blister. They would soon lose their motivation and would miss the blessing that was theirs all along.

One of the keys to using your faith is to know you have what God has promised and to keep after it until it manifests in the natural.

<u>Destined to Win</u>

**Thanks be unto God, which always causeth us
to triumph in Christ.**
2 Corinthians 2:14

I know I'm a winner. Does that mean I always win? Well, it means I have the capability of always winning. Sometimes I have quit in my physical self and haven't always seen things work out the way I would have liked, but I was still convinced that I was a winner. Losing didn't change the picture of who I am in Christ. If we take this scripture to heart and realize it is God who always causes us to triumph through our Lord Jesus Christ, we will know we are winners. I've seen it in the Word. I know this scripture is talking about my born-again self.

Situations often come against me that honestly look bigger than I am, and they are. They're bigger than my physical self and my emotional self, but not my spirit man. In my spirit, I know I can do all things through Christ who strengthens me (Phil. 4:13). Because of that knowledge, sometimes I have just gutted it out; when in the physical, natural realm; it looked like I should have quit. But I just couldn't quit, because I knew I was a winner. And, praise God, I've seen the victory come.

Understanding who you are in Christ, your true identity, is one of the greatest motivating factors in the Christian life.

When my wife and I first got started, we didn't know very much of the Word of God, but I had this revelation that I knew I was a winner. I knew I was destined to overcome. I knew that the works Jesus did, I could do also. I just didn't understand how to get it done. I hadn't heard "Copenhagen"—the teachings of Kenneth Copeland and Kenneth Hagin. I didn't understand the ways of faith. I didn't know about confessing the Word and many other things about the faith life, but I had it burned in my heart that as a Christian, I was a winner, a victor.

I saw great miracles in my ministry. I saw blind eyes and deaf ears opened and people raised from the dead. When I look back at it, I wonder how in the world I saw so much success in those areas. I didn't know what I know now, but the key was that I was convinced it would work. I just kept at it and kept at it. My motivation was the difference because I saw myself differently. I wasn't seeing myself as just a physical person—I saw myself as a new creature in Christ Jesus.

I ask you again: How do you see yourself? Do you see yourself filled with the mind of Christ enabling you to operate in His power and authority, or do you still see yourself as simply a sinner whose sins have been washed away? Purpose in your heart and in your mind to see yourself as being the righteousness of Christ. The divine wisdom of God is yours today and forever. You no longer have to submit to your carnal emotions.

God has given you everything you need to operate with your new mind so you can control your emotions through the power of the Holy Spirit. You may not see your circumstances change immediately, but remember who you are in Christ—a victor, an overcomer, and a winner. You are a new creature, empowered with the mind of Christ.

Chapter 9

Walking in the Spirit

Many Christians see themselves as having been forgiven of their sins at the point they made Jesus their Lord, so their past sins are dealt with. But from the point of salvation on, every time they sin or do something wrong, they consider that to be a new infraction between them and God, one that has to be repented of and put under the blood of Jesus so it can be cleansed and washed away. They believe that if they were to die without having confessed, repented, and been forgiven of their sin, they would go to hell in that sinful state.

That is a typical belief among many Pentecostals, but it simply is not what God's Word teaches. God's Word teaches that when we accepted Jesus as our Savior and Lord, we were *sanctified* and *perfected* forever. Our spirits were made perfect once and for all.

I have a relative who many years ago had a very rebellious daughter. She was always pushing her mother to the limits of tolerance. One evening as this woman was fixing supper, her daughter pushed her too far, and so she hauled off and hit her. She decked her own daughter right onto the kitchen floor.

She was so shocked at what she had done that she ran upstairs and threw herself across the bed. She cried out to God for help because she knew if she started crying, it would be the next morning before she could compose herself. Her husband was bringing people home for supper, and she had to pull herself together.

What the Lord spoke to her was amazing. He said, "When you asked Me to forgive you for your sins as an eight-year-old girl, I already knew about the sin you would commit today and forgave it too." What a word! The Lord didn't only forgive her of past and present sins at her salvation, but He also forgave her future sins.

Sealed with the Spirit

In whom [Christ] ye also trusted, after that ye heard the word of truth, the gospel of your salvation: in whom [Christ] also after that ye believed, ye were sealed with that holy Spirit of promise.
Ephesians 1:13, brackets mine

When we are born again, we are given brand-new spirits. We are new creatures—old things have passed away, all things have become new. We are now recreated in righteousness and true holiness. There is no sin and no impurity in our new spirits whatsoever, because at the moment of salvation, we were sealed with the Holy Spirit of promise.

Notice the word **"sealed"** used here in Ephesians 1:13. There are different types of seals. There is a seal like the one placed on the garden tomb where Jesus was buried after the crucifixion (Matt. 27:66). It was an insignia that would show if anyone moved the stone away from the entrance to the tomb, because the seal would be broken. There is also the seal of approval or certification, such as the *Good Housekeeping* Seal, which testifies that a certain product or service has been tested and shown to meet a certain standard of quality or excellence.

But when Paul says in Ephesians 1:13 that we have been sealed with the Holy Spirit of promise, the seal he is referring to is the kind of seal that is used when a person cans food. They put it in an airtight container and then place paraffin over the top to ensure that no air can get in. In this way, the contents are preserved, because the seal keeps out any impurities.

That is what happened to us when we were saved. The Holy Spirit sealed our salvation and completely encased our born-again spirits so no impurities could get in.

All of the scriptures we have examined thus far show that when we received our new spirits, they were given to us in righteousness and true holiness (Eph. 4:24)—sanctified and perfected forever (Heb. 10:10 and 14). Our spirits were immediately sealed so that regardless of how we might sin in our physical, emotional realm, that contamination would not get into our spiritual realm. Our spirits retain that holiness, allowing us to have a pure relationship with the Lord.

Our Spirits Are Made Perfect

But ye are come unto mount Sion, and unto the city of the living God, the heavenly Jerusalem, and to an innumerable company of angels,

To the general assembly and church of the firstborn, which are written in heaven, and to God the Judge of all, and to the spirits of just men made perfect.

Hebrews 12:22-23

A lack of understanding has caused many believers to experience the love of God and to be excited and joyful about their salvation when they are doing everything right, but when they sin, they hit the skids and go through the depths of depression, asking, "God, how could You love me?" They see themselves as sinful, contaminated, sorry, no good, worthless, and hopeless, and they think that's the way God sees them.

The writer of Hebrews says that the spirits of those who are in Christ have been made perfect. In John 4:24, Jesus said, **"God is a Spirit: and they that worship him must worship him in spirit and in truth."** Since God is a Spirit, we can only fellowship with Him through our spirits, which have been perfected for that very purpose.

> **For by grace are ye saved through faith; and that not of yourselves: it is the gift of God:**
> **Not of works, lest any man should boast.**
> **For we are his workmanship, created in Christ Jesus unto good works, which God hath before ordained that we should walk in them.**
> *Ephesians 2:8-10*

Our perfect spirits do not fluctuate based on our actions. As we see in this scripture, our spirits are totally God's workmanship created in Christ Jesus unto good works. As such, they are not dependent upon us or our personal purity or holiness. Because of what God has done for us in Jesus Christ, our spirits are righteous and holy in themselves, and they stay that way. Given our unchanging spiritual nature, even when we sin, we can still go to God and receive His love and acceptance because our spirits—the only part of us that is born again—are still righteous, holy, pure, and acceptable to God. They are not stained by our sin.

Does that mean it is immaterial whether we live a holy life or not? Does that mean we can choose to live in sin because our spirits are righteous? Absolutely not!

> **Know ye not, that to whom ye yield yourselves servants to obey, his servants ye are to whom ye obey; whether of sin unto death, or of obedience unto righteousness?**
> *Romans 6:16*

Even though our spirits are still righteous in the eyes of God and we are not contaminated in the born-again part of us, if we choose to live in sin, we are giving Satan access to us. When we yield to Satan, we yield ourselves to his control. He is then free to do with us whatever he wants. If we choose to give in to sin, our spirits will still retain their righteousness with God, but our emotions and our bodies will suffer because we have opened the door for Satan to steal, kill, and destroy (John 10:10).

It is very important to live a holy life. Why? So God will accept us? No, He has already done that through Jesus. Once we were born again, we became new creatures—sealed and perfected forever. But we still have physical bodies and an emotional realm that we cannot ignore. We are not only spirits, but we also have souls and bodies to maintain. Our emotions are in the soulish realm, so if we choose to live in sin, we are going to give Satan access to our emotions and our bodies. We will end up leading a miserable life even though, in our spirits, we are sanctified and made perfect in the eyes of God.

Free to Fellowship with God

Let us therefore come boldly unto the throne of grace, that we may obtain mercy, and find grace to help in time of need.
Hebrews 4:16

One of the biggest benefits of understanding our new identity in Christ is the recognition that our new person, our born-again selves, is now able to fellowship freely with God. Because our new spirits are His creation, they are righteous, holy, and pure, and there is nothing to condemn us or make us feel guilty or unworthy before Him. Our worthiness is not based on anything we have done, but solely on what Jesus has done for us. He has made us a new person. Once we understand that, it gives us boldness to enter into the very presence of God.

We can get rid of our guilt and condemnation—not by denying that they exist, and not by saying that it doesn't matter what we do with our minds and bodies because they are ours to do with as we please—but by becoming a new person in Christ. Regardless of what has happened to us in the past, or even what may be happening to us in the present, we can go before the Lord and say, "Father, thank You that I am still righteous in Your sight."

We don't confess our sin for the purpose of getting our spirits saved or born again, because that has already taken place. We have already received new spirits within us. It is a past-tense event that stays complete. They have been sealed forever. We confess our sin for the purpose of kicking Satan out of our lives. We gave place to him when we sinned. Now as we repent and confess that sin, we kick him out and receive the forgiveness that is already a reality in our spirits, bringing it out into the soulish and emotional part of us to set us free from depression, guilt, hatred, and bitterness—all of the negative things that sin brings to our emotions.

Isn't that powerful? God has already done everything in your spirit that needs to be done to save you from sin so you can live in holiness and fellowship with Him now and forever. You are righteous, you are holy, you are pure, and you always will be. That knowledge will give you stability in your Christian life. Your emotions won't be up or down based on your performance. Instead, your emotions will remain as stable and unchanging as your spirit.

Remember, your emotions are based on who you are in Christ. Even though your actions may fluctuate up and down, your emotions won't. Because of the knowledge you have within you, when you have failed in some way and see those emotions beginning to plummet, you will simply say, "Father, I'm sorry. I'm in the flesh. I'm doing wrong things, so I repent in Jesus' name."

When you get your mind off of who you are in yourself and put it back on who you are in Christ, your emotions will come right back to a level of peace and joy that are yours because of what Jesus has done for you. Everything will begin to become more stable, because you will be focusing more and more on the eternal things that are true on the inside of you rather than on your temporal, physical circumstances and emotions.

Walking out the New You

This understanding has transformed my life. There's no way I can share with you in this short book everything I have learned about this lifestyle, but during the more than forty years that the Lord has been teaching all this to me, I have been realizing that there is a totally new me on the inside. I have been developing a whole new attitude about myself. That may sound a little crazy to you at first. You may be asking yourself what planet I came from, because this new way of life is radically different compared to the thinking of this world.

Again, one of the major differences between psychology and true Christianity is that psychology doesn't tell you that you can become a new person. It doesn't tell you to see yourself in Christ Jesus. It doesn't tell you that you are righteous, holy, pure, and forgiven. Instead, it just takes your old self and tries to get you to feel good about it, to place the blame for your emotional problems on someone else, and to teach you how to deal with things from a merely human perspective.

What I am talking about is supernatural. It requires a revelation from God. It takes a miracle from God to make it a reality. But that's what Jesus came to do.

You are a totally brand-new person in your spirit. You are righteous, holy, and pure. God loves you. He is not displeased with you, not your new born-again self. I guarantee you there are things in your old, unregenerate self that God does not care a lick for, but your born-again self is totally brand-new, and you need to learn how to dwell in it. This is what the Bible calls "walking in the spirit."

This I say then, Walk in the Spirit, and ye shall not fulfil the lust of the flesh.

Galatians 5:16

Walking in the spirit does not mean walking in some weird posture, going around with your hands folded, saying "Hallelujah!" and looking "holier than thou." Walking in the spirit is simply believing what God's Word says about who you are in Christ. When you truly do that and walk in accordance with that revelation, you are walking in the spirit. That revelation of who you are in Christ becomes the way you think, the way you see yourself, and the way you act toward yourself and others.

But the fruit of the Sprit is love, joy, peace, longsuffering, gentleness, goodness, faith, Meekness, temperance: against such there is no law.

Galatians 5:22-23

This scripture tells you what is a reality in your spirit. In your emotions, you may not *feel* love, but the Bible says your spirit *is* love. What are you going to do about that truth? Are you going to go by what you feel in your emotions or by what God's Word says you have in your spirit?

Some people hear that and think, *But it would be hypocritical if I said that I have love, when the truth is that I feel hate.* It would be hypocritical *if* you think the physical fleshly part of you is the real you. If you consider that emotional part of you to be the real you, then it would be hypocritical to say you love someone when on the inside, you are ready to cut their gizzard out.

However, if you have come to realize that the real you is your spirit, the born-again part of you, it would be hypocritical for you to say you did not have love on the inside of you. Don't deny that the emotional, physical part of you exists, but it is not the real you. That's the old you. That's the way you were before you were born again. Although the physical part of you still exists, refuse to allow it to rule over you or dominate you. When you feel hatred for someone, that doesn't mean that like a hypocrite, you lie and say you love them. You simply recognize that the hatred you feel is evidence of the existence of the old, carnal thinking still within you. When you feel that emotion, it helps you to identify that you are walking in the flesh and need to get back into the spirit because in your spirit, you have God's love for that person.

Isn't that simple? The Christian life is so easy once we understand this principle, we have to have someone help us to misunderstand it. Sad to say, we've had more than enough help with our misunderstandings.

> **He that believeth on me, as the scripture hath said, of out of his belly shall flow rivers of living water.**
> **(But this spake he of the Spirit, which they that believe on him should receive: for the Holy Ghost was not yet given; because that Jesus was not yet glorified.)**
>
> *John 7:38-39*

Some people know that the Word of God says we are supposed to love our enemies, but they feel hatred, so they ask, "Lord, what's wrong with me?" Their problem is that they are trying to change their feelings and force the physical part of them to line up with the Word of God. It's never going to work.

When you find yourself in that kind of situation, you need to say, "Father, according to Galatians 5:22, the fruit of the Spirit is love. Because I have Your Spirit, I have that love, but at the moment, I'm not feeling it. That must mean I'm walking in the flesh, and I am letting my emotional, physical, soulish part dominate me." Then you should go to the Word of God and start reading and meditating on scriptures about love. You will see the spirit of love Jesus had in Him when He prayed for God to forgive those who crucified Him

(Luke 23:34). You will see the spirit of love that was in Stephen when he forgave those who stoned him to death (Acts 7:60). Then you can say, "I have that same spirit on the inside of me." Start thinking that way, and start seeing yourself as having the love of God within you. As you think on that and dwell on it, your emotions will begin to fall in line, and the love of God will begin to flow out of you, just as Jesus said it would.

Let the Spirit Man Rule

Many people don't know they have a choice about how to feel. They think, *If I feel depressed, that's the way it is. I can't help it.* But that's not true. Your born-again spirit is never depressed. It is always full of love, joy, peace, long-suffering, gentleness, goodness, faith, meekness, and temperance. Your spirit never gets depressed. Your spirit has never been down, defeated, sad, or self-pitying. The born-again part of you is always rejoicing in the Lord.

If you know that, then when depression comes your way, you will realize that you have a choice: Are you going to be dominated by our old, unregenerate emotions, or are you going to let your born-again feelings dominate you? Are you going to dwell on who you are in yourself and let your negative emotions make you miserable, or are you going to dwell on who you are in Christ and let the love and joy of His Spirit flow out of you?

Some of us have spent years in depression praying and asking God for help, and the help was within us all along. Our spirits were rejoicing, and if we had renewed our minds with what God's Word says and started thinking in line with it, we could have experienced that joy the whole time.

If that describes you, you have been asking God to give you something that you already have. How is God going to respond? Suppose you stood in front of me and asked me for my Bible.

Imagine that I handed it to you and said, "Here." Then, once you had it in your hand, you kept saying, "Would you please give me your Bible?" What could I do? How could I give you something you already had? I would probably look at you and wonder what's wrong with you.

That's the reason some of us have prayed: "O God, deliver me from depression." Then we wondered why we weren't getting an answer. God is wondering, *How do I respond? I've given them My life. What more can I do?*

The same joy you will have throughout all eternity is already on the inside of you. It's not a matter of going to God and getting something from Him; it's a matter of releasing something that's already there. You start doing that by seeing what God's Word says about who you are in Christ and then dwelling on it.

The Bible says that the first three fruit of the Spirit are love, joy, and peace. Start thanking God and praising Him for the fact that you already have these things, and they will start manifesting in your life. As your mind begins to be renewed and you choose to believe who you really are in Christ, then you will bring the things that are already there in your spirit out into the physical realm.

Your mind is the key. As you renew your mind, these things that are in the spirit will manifest themselves in the soulish, emotional realm. You will experience the peace that goes with the love and joy that are in your spirit, and you will be on your way to letting the Holy Spirit within you rule and reign over every part of your life.

<u>Dying to the Flesh</u>

You may have love, joy, and peace, but what about long-suffering? When you get angry at someone, your spirit is not short-fused. Your spirit is capable of operating in long-suffering, gentleness, faith, meekness, temperance, and all of the other fruit of the Spirit.

If you are battling something like your weight or your eating habits and you say "I just can't seem to control myself," you just identified your problem. You are operating in the flesh, because the spirit has temperance. You're right; you cannot control your *self*. But the spirit is able to discipline the flesh. Your spirit isn't dominated by lust and desire.

The answer is simply to say, "Father, I'm sorry. I'm operating in the flesh again." Repent and start thinking and meditating on who you are in Christ, thanking God that you have His life and His Spirit on the inside of you. Your spirit is able to control what you eat. As you begin to think that way, your emotions and actions will begin to follow.

You are already a complete person in Christ Jesus. You don't need any improvement. When you go to be with the Lord, your spirit isn't going to have to be dusted off. You won't have to be changed, refurbished, patched up, or plugged up. Your spirit is sanctified, perfected, and sealed. It's holy. It's pure. There's nothing wrong there. That makes it so easy to walk in the spirit.

Go to God's Word, and find out what your spirit is really like. Then realize that that is who you are. Anytime you feel or act contrary to your spirit, you are in the flesh. All you have to do is say, "No wonder I'm having problems. The reason I'm not experiencing love, joy, peace, long-suffering, or any of the other fruit of the Spirit is because I'm in the flesh."

Now, you may be thinking, *But it's natural for me to react the way I do—just look at what I'm going through.* If it's *natural*, that's the flesh. Your born-again self is not natural; it's *supernatural*. It is totally the workmanship of God. When you find yourself operating in the natural and in the flesh, you need to repent. Quit trying to improve your old, dead flesh. Instead, change your perception of your new, redeemed self. Begin to confess, "I'm not going to be that old man anymore. Even though these things come against me, they don't bother me. If I forget and get angry, I don't get upset. I don't feel condemned. I don't get discouraged."

If someone does you wrong, don't get into self-pity or anger. As soon as you start having thoughts like that, say, "Whoops, that's the flesh. That's my old self, because my born-again self doesn't get offended or indulge in self-pity." Then turn to the Lord and say, "Father, forgive me for getting into the flesh. I haven't been meditating on You. I haven't been thinking on what I should. I have been operating in the flesh, living in the natural realm, listening to the wrong things, thinking the wrong thoughts. And here I am, reaping the results. So I repent."

Get into the Word. That's what I do. I start praying and meditating on who I am and thinking about what God has done for me. And do you know what happens? Love begins to flow through me instead of anger. Joy begins to flow through me instead of depression. Peace and long-suffering start flowing through me instead of worry and anxiety. It happens every time.

Let the Peace of God Rule

Let the peace of God rule in your hearts.
Colossians 3:15

Some people have trouble recognizing whether or not they are flowing in the spirit, or whether they are doing the right thing or not. That is easily determined. Your spirit always has love, joy, peace, long-suffering, and all the other fruit of the Spirit. Your flesh very seldom has these things. Paul gives us the answer in Colossians 3:15: **"Let the peace of God rule in your hearts."** Now, this takes awhile to experience. It takes some growth. You have to mature so you are able to distinguish between the things of the flesh and the things of the spirit.

In doubtful situations, consider your options. If you have worry, fear, or anxiety within, that is the flesh. But if you have peace within, a peace that you may not understand, a peace that may not make sense to you, a peace that you may not be able to prove to anyone else, that is the spirit.

> **Let the peace (soul harmony which comes) from Christ rule (act as umpire continually) in your hearts [deciding and settling with finality all questions that arise in your minds, in that peaceful state] to which as [members of Christ's] one body you were also called [to live]. And be thankful (appreciative), [giving praise to God always].**
> *Colossians 3:15, AMP*

You may have questions. Your peace may not be 100 percent because you are not yet 100 percent in tune to your spirit. But once you discern that peace, let it rule. Let it overcome any objection, just as an umpire makes a call and sticks with it. Let your peace have the final say. Follow that peace and you will be following your spirit man.

You walk in the spirit as you walk in the peace of God, and as you do so, it becomes a tremendous influence in your life.

Emotional Stability Guaranteed

> **Believing, ye rejoice with joy unspeakable and full of glory.**
> *1 Peter 1:8*

This verse is saying that when we are in faith, the emotion of joy unspeakable and full of glory follows. If that joy isn't present, it's because we are believing or focusing on something other than what God's Word says about our born-again selves. We're in unbelief instead of faith.

There is so much more to share on this subject, but I believe I have laid the foundation. I encourage you to go to God's Word and start discovering your true identity, finding out who you are in Christ. As you do that and begin to renew your mind; focusing it on the new, born-again you; you will bring those things that are already true in your spirit out into the physical, emotional realm. According to how you think, your emotions will follow. As you think in your heart, so are you (Prov 23:7). That's the way it is, and the way it will always be. If you are spiritually minded, it will produce life and peace (Rom. 8:6). If you keep your mind stayed upon the Lord, He will keep you in perfect peace (Is. 26:3). It's just that simple.

Meditate on these truths until you get the proper self-image, which is the revelation of who you are in Christ. Focus your attention and base your life on that concept. Your emotions and your actions will never be the same again.

Conclusion

We were created with emotions and have been given the power through Jesus Christ to control them. We are to accept that responsibility and learn how to properly release those emotions. The answer to harnessing our emotions is not found in the world's psychology but rather by choosing to apply the Word of God in faith. We need to look at your circumstances and situations in the light of eternity, and we will see they are only for a moment. We are more than conquerors over everything the world throws our way, and we need to begin seeing ourselves that way.

Psychology tries to help us develop a good self-image to make us feel good about ourselves. That concept can provide some immediate relief, but it is not the answer, and self will ultimately fail. We are to find our self-esteem in Jesus, which means denying our own selves, taking up our cross daily, and following Him.

If you have read this book but still don't truly know the Lord Jesus Christ in a personal way, the principles I have set forth will not work for you, except to a limited degree. You may experience some relief, but just being positive in your thinking is not the answer to your deepest need, which is to become a new person in Christ and receive His life in your spirit. If you aren't a totally new person, then regardless of how positive your thinking is, it won't change anything.

Positive thinking is not the answer—**"You must be born again"** (John 3:7, NIV).

You may already believe that Jesus Christ exists, but have you ever committed yourself to Him and trusted Him one hundred percent? If you were to stand before God right now and He asked you "What makes you worthy?" would you point to yourself? Would you point to your morality, to your actions, or to how good you have been? Or would you point to Jesus and say, "I am trusting

Him"? Romans 3:23 says that all have sinned and come short of the glory of God. Everyone needs a Savior.

If you have never made Jesus Christ your personal Lord and Savior, you need to make a commitment to Him today. Do as the Scripture says: Confess with your mouth and believe in your heart that Jesus is Lord and that God raised Him from the dead, and you will be saved (Rom. 10:9). That means more than just acknowledging that He exists or that He was a historical figure; it means committing yourself to Him, making Him your Lord and Master, Ruler of your life. It means putting your faith in Him to save you from your sin and to direct your life now and forever.

When you do that, a transformation takes place on the inside—you become a brand-new person. You may not feel it physically, because the actual new birth is not something you feel. It can't be proven based on feelings; it is something that is taken by faith in God.

When you commit yourself to God and to His Word—reading it, understanding it, and living it—this new life will begin to manifest itself in your emotions and in your physical body. You will have victory over your emotions by choosing to rejoice in the Lord despite your circumstances, trusting Him to bring you through whatever comes your way in this life.

Pray the following prayer in simple faith, and you will become a brand-new person, a brand-new creature in Christ Jesus.

"Father, I acknowledge that I've sinned and cannot save myself. Jesus is my only hope of salvation. Right now, I put my faith in Him. I make Jesus Christ my Savior and Lord. I believe that You have forgiven me all my sins. I believe that Jesus is alive from the dead and that He now comes and lives in me so I can become a new person in Him. I believe it and I thank You for it in the name of Jesus. Amen."

If you prayed that prayer with your mouth and meant it in your heart, then that spiritual transformation has taken place on the inside of you. You are now born again. You are a brand-new person—a totally new creature. The rest of the Christian life is learning to understand what has taken place within you and living it out day by day.

Now that you have made that decision for Christ, you need to begin renewing your mind. Start identifying with who you are in Christ, esteeming Him on the inside, and recognizing that He has given you control over your emotions. You can then live in peace of mind and heart, rejoicing with joy unspeakable and full of glory.

About the Author

Andrew Wommack was brought up in a Christian home in Arlington, Texas, and made a total commitment of his life to the Lord at a very early age. But it was not until he received the baptism of the Holy Spirit as a teenager that he began to experience the power of God in his life.

For over three decades, he has traveled America and the world teaching the truth of the Gospel. His profound revelation of the Word of God is taught with clarity and simplicity, emphasizing God's unconditional love and the balance between grace and faith. He reaches millions of people through the daily *Gospel Truth* radio and television programs, broadcast both domestically and internationally. He founded Charis Bible College in 1994 and has since established CBC extension schools in other major cities of America and around the world. Andrew has produced a library of teaching materials, available in print, audio, and visual formats. And, as it has been from the beginning, his ministry continues to distribute free audio materials to those who cannot afford them.

To contact Andrew Wommack, please write, email, or call:

Andrew Wommack Ministries
P.O. Box 3333 • Colorado Springs, CO 80934-3333
Email: info@awmi.net
Helpline Phone (orders and prayer): 719-635-1111
Hours: 4:00 AM to 9:30 PM MST

Andrew Wommack Ministries of Europe
P.O. Box 4392 • WSI 9AR Walsall • England

Or visit him on the web:
www.awmi.net

Other Teachings
By Andrew Wommack

The New You & The Holy Spirit

What really happened when you were saved and filled with the Holy Spirit? Read as Andrew gives you the specifics of your new life in Christ and the Baptism of the Holy Spirit.

Item Code: 323   Paperback

The Effects of Praise

The effects that praise can cause are unstoppable! The devil runs, unbelief leaves the heart, and God is blessed!

Item Code: 1004-C   3-CD album
Item Code: 309   Paperback

Discover the Keys to Staying Full of God

Staying full of God is not a secret or mysterious; it's simple. For that reason, few people recognize the keys, and even less practice them. Learn what they are and put them into practice; they will keep your heart sensitive.

Itcm Code: 1029-C   4-CD album
Item Code: 1029-D   DVD album
Item Code: 324   Paperback
Item Code: 424   Study Guide

The True Nature of God
Understanding the Word of God begins with understanding the nature of God. Get that wrong and Scripture will never make sense!

Item Code: 1002-C   5-CD album
Item Code: 308   Paperback

Spirit, Soul & Body
Understanding the relationship of your spirit, soul, and body is foundational to your Christian life. You will never be able to relate to God properly without it!

Item Code: 1027-C   4-CD album
Item Code: 1027-D   DVD album
Item Code: 318   Paperback
Item Code: 418   Study Guide

You've Already Got It!
Are you trying to get God to heal, bless, deliver, or prosper you? If so, stop it! God has already done all He will ever do for you. Andrew explains these truths in this teaching.

Item Code: 1033-C   6-CD album
Item Code: 320   Paperback

A Better Way to Pray
The principles found in this teaching may not be the only way to pray, but if you are not getting the results you desire, consider that there could be *A Better Way to Pray*.

Item Code: 1042-C   4-CD album
Item Code: 1042-D   DVD album
Item Code: 321   Paperback

Insights into Faith

For many, faith is elusive. Some seem to have it and others don't. The Bible says we all have "the measure of faith" (Rom. 12:3). Read and Andrew will explain.

Item Code: 100   Mini Booklet

Grace, the Power of the Gospel

The vast majority of Christians believe their salvation is at least in part dependent on their performance. Paul's revelation of grace in Romans settles the issue. It's not what you do, but what Jesus did.

Item Code: 1014-C   4-CD album
Item Code: 1014-D   DVD album
Item Code: 322   Paperback
Item Code: 422   Study Guide

The War Is Over

Many have not heard the news that the longest conflict in history ended in a decisive victory nearly 2,000 years ago. They continue to fight the battle of sin and judgment. This teaching will set you free from condemnation, judgment, and fear so you can receive the blessings of God.

Item Code: 1053-C   5-CD album
Item Code: 326   Paperback
Item Code: 426   Study Guide